Joe,
Hope you enjoy
the book.
Thanks,
Bob Bracken

The Speed-Shift King
and Other
Revoltin' Developments

Bob Bracken

PublishAmerica
Baltimore

First printing

ISBN: 978-1-4489-9615-5
PUBLISHED BY PUBLISHAMERICA, LLLP
www.publishamerica.com
Baltimore

Printed in the United States of America

Dedication

This book is dedicated to; my wife Bev, my sons Bobby and Jeff, my granddaughters Jessie, Alyssa and Amanda and daughter-in laws, Lisa and Fany and to all of my friends mentioned in these stories, who I can't imagine having grown up without; even the guys that used to beat me up.

Also to my late friend Richard Prince who inspired me to put these stories in print in the first place.

Acknowledgements

Thanks to Megan Bennet, Michael Zedack, John A. Mcdonald, Richard Brightly,The late Richard Prince, Steve and Jody for input, encouragement illustrations, photos, etc.

The Speed-Shift King and Other Revoltin' Developments

By Bob Bracken 2009

The stories contained in this book are actual, and the people depicted in them are real. Some embellishment was added for the sake of humor, but not much was needed, as the events described within this book are humorous enough in their own right. Although it might not have seemed so, in some of the incidents, at the time.

The time-line of the stories depicted within this book are between the mid-nineteen fifties and the mid-nineteen sixties. This time period was probably one of the best times to be growing up in America, especially if you happened to be a "motor-head." But being a motor-head certainly wasn't a prerequisite for enjoying the prosperous, innocent post World War Two era that, unfortunately, will not in all likely-hood, ever be experienced again. Stories similar to the ones in this book happened all over America at the time.

Kids made their own fun during these years, and friends were very important as there was no internet or instantly satisfying electronic games to occupy ones-self. Almost everything we did, we did outside, with our friends, winter or summer.

The stories are about typical adolescent life in that wonderful era, and what we did day to day to pass the time, making our own fun, which, at times, had negative consequences. We learned how to deal with obstacles; we learned how to deal with bullies, (it was often a daily goal trying to not get your ass kicked). We customized our bicycles, and envied the older guys in town that owned their own cars, watching and emulating every move they made. Eventually all this led up to the ultimate, much anticipated life-changing event of getting our own driver's license which brought with it the freedom to go where we wanted, when we wanted. We never realized at the time, that this was just the start of a life-time of ever increasing personal responsibilities, and we were really leaving our actual freedom behind.

The wholesomeness and work ethic of the 1930s and 40s was still alive in the nineteen fifties and nineteen sixties. People, as a rule, had more money to spend during these flourishing times, and the automobile manufacturers did everything they could to entice the public to buy their product, from ostentatious designs and colors to high-performance factory race-ready cars and we all yearned to be a part of this world on wheels.

The stories within are fact-based from actual experiences of the author and his friends in the North Jersey City of Clifton, New Jersey, and primarily in the unique, blue-collar, working-class section of Clifton called Delawanna; aptly named for the Delaware and Lackawanna Railroad that ran through the heart of little town with the "wrong side of the tracks" reputation, which, by the way, it did not deserve…well, maybe just a little!

Chapter One:
Birthday Surprises One Good, One Bad

Saturday March 13, 1955 was my tenth birthday and I awoke earlier than usual with great anticipation as to what I might be getting as a present. All I really wanted was a U.S. Army surplus flashlight. The olive drab colored plastic type with the 90 degree head. I knew the model number was TL-122D from studying the ones that were for sale at Curry's Army and Navy Surplus Store in Passaic, NJ. Curry's had large wooden bins filled with all kinds of U.S. Military surplus items and this flashlight was one of the items I just had to have in my growing collection of military accoutrements.

My friend Roy's father, Mr. Dickson, would take us to Curry's almost whenever we asked to go. He was a World War Two veteran and enjoyed looking at all the military items and telling us what they were used for. We were into anything related to the U.S. Army and saved our pennies to buy items like; canteens, ammo belts, leggings, etc. . Anyway, I really wanted this particular flashlight as a tactical aid should we be attacked by the Japanese or German Army. If that were to happen Roy and I would have to signal each other as to our tactics in quelling any such attacks from any foes, foreign or domestic and, in general, just to assist us in thwarting the forces of evil, of which, we were convinced, there were many, at least in our over active imaginations there were.

So I made sure my parents knew exactly which flashlight I wanted. It had to be the TL-122D, because it was the improved model and had the extended base with the very essential different color lens filters in the base compartment. These colored lenses were definitely needed for secret communications if we were going to be effective in our National Security efforts!

I thought I had a pretty good chance of getting this item as it sold for only $1.50 or so. However, considering that my father made approximately that amount per hour at Curtiss-Wright in Fairfield, New Jersey, maybe it would not be in the budget.

When I came downstairs for breakfast that day my mother greeted me with a "happy birthday" greeting and also a birthday card signed; Love Mom, Dad and guess who? The guess who was easy to figure out because it was a dogs paw print transferred to the card by the using a burned cork that was applied to the paw of my black and white Fox Terrier mix "Trixie"; Named after Art Carney's character, (Ed Norton's) wife Trixie from Jackie Gleason's "Honeymooners" Show.

My mother asked if I wanted pancakes for breakfast on this special day as it was always one of my favorites; Especially when she covered them with her home-made peach preserves. However, I declined and asked for a bowl of Cheerios instead. I was trying to be loyal to Cheerios, because The Lone Ranger and Tonto said they were good for you, and I figured if the Lone Ranger and Tonto ate them, then I would eat them also. Of course, it never occurred to me back then that the time-line between the Lone Ranger's lifetime, which was depicted sometime in the late 1800s, and Cheerios, which wasn't introduced until the 1940s, was off by at least sixty years. No way did the Lone Ranger ever eat Cheerios! In fact, as I think about it now, there was a greater likelihood that he probably ate pancakes with peach preserves!

Advertising was very easy to aim at young boys by using their heroes as a lure.

Wild Bill Hickok and his partner "Jingles" used to tout the virtues of eating Grape-Nuts or Post Toasties and how those cereals helped them fight the bad guys. When I think of it now, Jingles' poor old horse "Joker" was the one that needed the extra energy, just to carry the grossly overweight Jingles (played by Andy Devine) around! He had to be 80lbs overweight, but they had my friends and me convinced that he could tangle with the best of them…and win!

Anyway, Dad was at work this day at Wrights trying to make an extra buck to get ahead, which never seemed to happen as he was always either getting laid-off or they were on strike. The end of the war caused huge financial woes for Wrights and they were always having some sort of labor issue at that time it seemed.

Dad worked in the propeller department at Wrights and he used to tell me about the gas powered floor sweeper they had there, because he knew how much I liked anything with wheels. He used to tell me that when I was old enough, he would try to get me a job driving it. I said, "Tell them I'll do it for free!"

At that particular time in my life the only experience I had in driving anything with an engine in or on it was when I drove my Uncle Albert's tractor into a ditch the previous summer!

That incident occurred when my mother and I along with my aunt, uncle and two cousins went to visit my mother's family in Fisherville, Ontario, Canada. While there I was allowed to drive an uncle's Oliver Standard 80 tractor to less than rave reviews. As I attempted to back up on the front farm road, I rolled it into a ditch! Not a good thing to do on a tractor as they tend to very easily flip-over backwards in these situations. I was relegated to the horse-drawn hay wagon after that incident. I guess they figured the horse was smarter and would correct any errors in judgment on my part!

Back to my birthday breakfast. After I scoffed down two bowls of Cheerios Mom placed a wrapped box in front of me at the table and said, "Happy Birthday!" I quickly tore off the wrapping and opened the box, *Yes*...it was a TL-122D 90 degree United States Army flashlight! *Wow!* This is great! I have to tell Roy right away! Mom told me it was too early to run next door (we shared a duplex home with the Dicksons). So, I ran upstairs and banged on the wall that separated his house and bedroom from mine. We used to talk through the wall all the time at night and when the weather was warm, we would both climb out of our bedroom windows and sit on the connected roofs. In the summer we would always light punks (that we picked down at the pond across from our home and then dried up on the same roof) to keep the mosquitoes away. Anyway, I contacted Roy through the wall and he said he would meet me in my backyard in ten minutes...after his Cheerios, of course!

We met in my back-yard in full battle-dress as usual, ready to defend our domain no-matter-what. Only this time my confidence in our ability to take on enemies and intruders was extremely high because I had my brand-new TL-122D 90 degree flashlight hooked to my ammo belt. The fact that it was day-light and the flashlight was of no consequence didn't even enter my thoughts. Although we looked like fully-equipped infantry-men, we had not a single weapon between us. Among our accouterments and fastened to our bodies via ammo belt or knapsack was a variety of items purchased from Curry's such as: a canteen filled with Kool-aid (not sure if real infantry-men had Kool-aid) a mess-kit, a folding drinking cup, water purifying pills (who needs that when you already have a canteen full of Kool-aid?), a Necco Skybar, a Clark Bar and some Black Jack chewing gum. Actually, as I think about it, we were fully equipped for eating and drinking, and not so much for fighting.

This day however, the Tl-122D made all the difference to us. It would even be better, we thought, when Roy got one, so I would have someone to actually signal to! With all of the items we carried, along with a vivid ten-year-old boy's imagination, we felt invincible. I mean, we believed the Lone Ranger and Tonto actually ate Cheerios and that overweight Jingles, good guy that he was, could take down any bad guys because he ate Grape Nuts, then so could we because we ate the same things that they ate.

Not allowing the fact we carried no weapons hinder our mission, Roy and I headed for the vast wooded area surrounding the "Yantacaw Pond" (it's proper Native Indian given name) or, the "Old Pond" as it was referred to by us. The "New Pond," a man-made pond, was just above the Old Pond off the west-bound lanes of Route # 3.

The old Pond was closer to the size of a small lake than it was a pond and the wooded area surrounding it stretched from Main Ave., in the Delawanna section of Clifton, NJ, to River Rd. and beyond. The entire area was approximately a mile long and quarter mile wide. Pretty good size woods for a city only twelve miles from New York City...even in those days.

The old Pond was fed by the "Third River" which flowed over the waterfall called the "18" for reasons unknown to me. From there the river came to an area called the "thousand roots," which is named for an ancient old tree that had near that many roots reaching out into the waterway from the banks along it's sides

The thousand roots was a place we used to go skinny-dipping at times until we saw two black men that used to fish there haul in a huge snapping turtle one day. They showed us how nasty those turtles were when one of the guys put a stick near the turtles mouth and he snapped it clean off! That sight sent fear through our bones at the thought of the parts of our anatomy that could easily meet the same fate! That pretty much ended any more skinny-dipping in that area, at least for me.

The waterway flowed from that point to an area that was called the "log jam," due to the amount of trees and broken limbs that restricted the water flow and created a small flood-pond. From there it made a ninety degree turn and followed William Street eastward behind the homes on the south side of the street, most of which had a foot-bridge to cross over the waterway. As it proceeded further along and deepened, boat docks with small row boats or canoes tied up were a common sight behind the homes on the south side of William Street.

Once the waterway cleared "Goldies Creek" (the deepest part of the creek named for the Goldie Carps (part Gold fish, part Carp) it emptied into the Old Pond and eventually ran over the Waldrich Bleachery falls, then down a canal and into the Passaic River, which ultimately emptied into the Newark Bay.

At any rate we were fortunate enough to have this large parcel of nature, along with several other large, woodlands and fields to play, hunt, fish, boat and swim in. Compared to the rest of the City of Clifton, we felt like we lived in the wilderness.

Back to our excursion from the safety and well-being of our homes on William St., and into the possible danger of unknown enemies that may lurk behind every tree in the woods. We were feeling pretty secure with the equipment we had, which included canvas Army issue leggings to protect our lower extremities from sticker bushes etc., which we purposely walked through to show

how well protected we were. There was one enemy, however, that we didn't count on, and were not prepared for…"poison ivy"!

The problem with poison ivy is that it takes a day-or-so of incubation after initial contact before it manifests itself. So, during the first time you came in contact with it (usually you weren't even aware of it) or during the germination period, you usually did nothing to prevent the spread of the, first itchy and then very sore rash that would soon become a major source of irritation.

Now, if you got infected by it, your mother would cover you with the pink medicine made specifically for it; "Calamine Lotion." Now with the application of Calamine Lotion everyone knew you had, *Poison Ivy* and no one would come near you because it was contagious! But, the biggest problem you faced was if you happened to relieve yourself while down in the woods after your initial contact with the dreaded three shiny-leafed, plant. Have you ever had Calamine Lotion on your "tally whacker"? Not good I can tell you…not good at all! Especially when it dries up, and starts to pull on the tender skin in that region. It felt like you had a rose bush in your underwear! It was a dreaded infection. The Coasters even recorded a song about the affects of poison ivy; *"you're gonna need an ocean…of calamine lotion!* . Having already been schooled in what to look for in regards to poisonous plants etc., Roy and I kept focused on other enemies and on this day we, unfortunately for us, found one in the form of one Russell Burgess.

Now Russ wasn't a soldier from a foreign country, and at times (usually when his mother was near) he wasn't even considered an enemy at all. Russ was three or four years older than Roy and me, so we were a little afraid and very wary of him as he was, at that time, one of the "semi-bullies" from Delawanna. Not one of the worst ones, but at times he could be a bully in sort of a mischievous Eddie Haskell (Leave it to Beaver) sort of way, at least to us he was. There were other times though, when he would play ball or some other sport with us.

It was always good if someone from outside Delawanna was around when Russ was in the "bullying" mood, as they would then get the brunt of any bullying that was to be dealt out.

However, on this day it was just Roy and me in the woods when we happened to come across Russ with, unfortunately... *his bow and arrow!!* Oh shit! This is not the enemy we were expecting to run in to. We thought perhaps a German or Japanese soldier left over from, and still fighting "the war." That scenario we were prepared for, but we were not prepared for Russ Burgess! Also, there was no one with him that could, or would talk him out of any mis-deeds he might have had in mind! At the time, it certainly didn't look like the TL-122D, or the two bowls of Cheerios I had eaten were going to do much to change the situation at hand! I thought to myself, I should have had the freakin' pancakes, at least I would die with something that tasted good in my stomach! What to do? Roy says, "Lets run!" I said, "Run? How are we going to run with all this crap from Curry's us weighing us down?!" "Knap-saks, ammo belts, canteens. Forget it, we are screwed, blued and double tattooed!" "Wait!Canteens...that's it, lets see if he wants some of our Kool-aid," I said. Roy then reminded me of the time Ted offered Russ a Kool-aid and Russ dumped it over his head!

Well, it was too late because he was ordering us to stay where we were and he then proceeded to walk over to us. When he reached our location he asked, "What are you two dorks doing down here with all that stupid shit on?"

Analyzing his question at the time, I deducted that it didn't sound good that he was calling us "dorks" right-off-the-bat. Nope...not a good start to our chance encounter with Russ. I thought, what would the Lone Ranger do if he encountered someone with a bow and arrow and then I realized that his side-kick, Tonto always had a bow and arrow. This analyzing was not helping us at the present time.

The bow Russ had was a lemon-wood, long-bow with the "Indian" brand decal on the front upper limb of the bow. I was familiar with this brand of bow and I had intended to buy one very soon myself, provided I survived this current situation, that is. Russ also had a quiver full of "field-tip" arrows. This (the field-tipped arrows) would turn out to be a blessing in disguise with-in the next few moments, as you will see. It soon became very apparent to Roy and me that Russ was, unfortunately for us, in one of his mischievous-bullying moods.

He walked around us making fun of all the military equipment we had on and asked, "Are you dorks expecting trouble or are you going to have a cook-out?" Now there was that word "dork" again. I mean, he hardly every called us by our given names anyway, but the name "dork" seemed like the prelude to bad behavior on Russ' part.

I tried to distract his thoughts from whatever they might have been, as most likely they were not good…for us that is! I told him I wanted to get a bow like his very soon. Then Roy said, "He might even get one today, because today is his birthday!" Oh no! I thought. Why did he tell him that?! I looked at Roy and he looked back and raised his eyebrows and shrugged his shoulders in an apologetic motion. Too late now! You never told someone like Russ it was your birthday!

"Oh really?," Russ said. Then he asked, "And just how old is the little dork today?" I nervously told him I was "ten." Russ then said we had to commemorate my birthday somehow. Then he told me to spread my feet two feet apart. I asked why, and he walked up closer and said, "Because I told you to, that's why!" With the fear of knowing I couldn't out-run him with all this crap on, I complied and spread my feet apart as directed.

Russ then said, "Now we are going to celebrate your birthday" and nocked an arrow, took aim, and shot the arrow between my feet! I started pleading with him not to do it! I even called "finsies" but to no avail (calling fins or finsies was supposed to bring a stop whatever negative thing was about to happen; a temporary sanctuary or diplomatic immunity of sorts) he completely ignored me, nocked up a second arrow and shot it between my feet again, right next to the first one! "Pretty good shootin' huh?" he asked in a rhetorical way. I nervously responded "Yes, but no more please." He completely ignored my plea and continued to shoot seven more arrows between my spread apart feet. Then he said. "That's ten for your age, but we need one more for good measure!" One more I thought, I didn't need any of them at all to start with!

Well, Russ drew back his bow string and shot the eleventh arrow, but this one did not bury itself in the frost-cover ground between my feet. No, not this time, my luck had run out (actually my luck ran out when we first encountered Russ) this one went right through my almost new, one week old "Red Ball Jets" sneaker on my right foot!! (The same Red Ball Jets that helped make me a "Junior Space Commander") Russ yelled, "Holy shit!" then reached down and collected all his arrows, all but the one imbedded in my right sneaker and said, "Sorry about that…you better not tell anyone or I'll beat the shit out of you." He then ran off through the woods in the direction of his home. Not tell anyone?! How the Hell was I not going to tell anyone? I had an arrow in my foot! However, I didn't feel any pain at this point and couldn't figure out why not.

Roy yanked the arrow out and I removed my sneaker, fearful of what I was going to see. Fortunately for me, the field tipped arrow managed to go in between my big toe and the one next to it! It only left small scrap marks on the skin where as it wedged it's way through. Wow! What luck! If this was a broad-head hunting tip, it wouldn't have fit between my toes and most likely would have severed one or both of them. But I still did have an arrow hole in my new sneaker! I had to tell my mother something when I got home. How could I hide it? What else could I have said caused this puncture in my sneaker?

Roy and I went back home and I decided to tell my mother exactly what happened as they (mothers) always seemed to find out the truth anyway. She took the arrow I still had with me and snapped it in two and then marched (that's what mothers did back then when they were on a mission…they marched!) down the street in the direction of Russ' house, which was on the same street that I lived on, but two blocks west of me.

When she returned home she told me that Mrs. Burgess grabbed Russ by the ear and brought him to her where he apologized profusely and promised to pay for my sneakers. That was it as far as that incident went. People were able to handle things like that between themselves back in those days.

I really didn't need any help in getting injured from Russ or anyone for that matter as I was more than capable of handling that task myself. Like the time I got wet swinging across the creek with a rope thrown over a large tree. After getting soaked, we lit a fire and I tried to dry off. The problem is, I stood too close to the fire and my pants caught on fire causing third degree burns to my left leg requiring a hospital stay. So, I really didn't need Russ adding to my propensity for getting injured.

Russ and I laugh about this and other incidents when we reminisce about them all these years later. Russ' response today when we bust his chops about bullying us back then is, "Yeah, but I stopped doing that as soon as you guys got bigger than me!" Russ is actually a very funny guy and is now very trustful and responsible with a bow and arrow.

Chapter Two:
The Green Hornet vs. The Blue Panther and Twin Problems

My faith in products supported by childhood heroes such as; The Lone Ranger and Tonto was still undaunted due to the wild imagination of a ten-year old boys' mind. I bought into all of the misconceptions of all the super-human strength and agility that could be gained by eating what my childhood heroes said were good for you. The problem is when one of your heroes is a dog named Farfel! I actually listened to a dog; not even a real dog mind you, but a dog puppet! However, when Jimmy Nelson's puppet Farfel sang; *N-E-S-T-L-E-S*, Nestles makes the very best, *CHOOOOCOLAAATE*, it made you ask your Mom to please buy some, which she always did.

Quaker Oats had the best gimmick to sell their product. First of all they used Sgt. Preston of the Yukon and his trusty Husky, Yukon King as the attraction. They also offered, in every box of Puffed Wheat or Puffed Rice, an actual deed to one square inch of Yukon Territory land! I had collected approximately twenty square inches of Yukon land in a short period of time. It was easy, because eating Puffed Wheat or Puffed Rice was the equivalent of eating Chinese food today. You always felt hungry, because it was like eating 50% air, so, naturally, you ate more of it, which was probably the general idea to start with.

My friends and I thought we could put our chunks of land together and possibly have enough land to build a cabin on. Yep, that's what I wanted to do; Move away from the warmth and comfort of our New Jersey home and live in a place that had six months of day-light and six months of darkness and most of the time it was freezing cold and filled with Grizzly Bears! I would rather deal with Russ Burgess than all of that, at least Russ Burgess was afraid of his mother and mine.

We thought we could actually help Sgt. Preston and Yukon King in their dealings with Klondike criminals. It had to be better than going to school, we thought, which was another childhood misconception. Nothing is better than school, you just don't realize it until it's too late.

That's how advertising gimmicks worked on ten-year olds. In retrospect, I guess I should be thankful I'm not being taxed on the land I owned in the Yukon.

Advertising even got me to eat Shredded Wheat…*YUK!* Shredded Wheat was supposed to be the most nutritious cereal/food you could eat and would definitely enhance your physical ability; especially when dealing with bullies. Unless, of course, the bullies also ate Shredded Wheat!

Shredded Wheat to a ten-year old, was the equivalent of eating burnt grass. It required so much milk, sugar, honey or syrup just to get it down that you were probably better off having a Snickers or Milky Way candy bar for breakfast. It had all the appeal of, what I imagined eating a wet Herald News newspaper would be like. But, I still forced it down, all the while hoping Russ Burgess wasn't.

As I stated before, Russ was not one of the real, feared bullies in Delawanna due to his Eddie Haskell-like personality; No, that distinction was reserved for one Jimmy Rau, a.k.a., "Pussy-Foot." Now here was, to us younger kids at least, a bully in every sense of the word, at least in our immature ten-year-old minds he was. Even Russ Burgess and other semi bullies were afraid of Pussy-Foot! He even looked mean with his dark, pronounced brow. It made him look perpetually mad, at least to us it did.

Pussy-Foot was about five or six years older than my friends and me and he rode around town on a Schwinn "Blue Panther" bicycle; That is, if he wasn't riding around on your bicycle, you know, the one he just took from you!

I don't know how he got the nick-name of Pussy-foot, but we, my friends and I, certainly didn't call him that and I was not about to ask him how he got it. Only his friends were permitted to call him Pussy-Foot. Besides, with my luck and being as nervous around him as I was, I might have stuttered and only got out the first part of his name! That would be a very bad thing! Shredded Wheat or no Shredded Wheat!

Well, back to the rest of my birthday on March 13, 1955. I survived the encounter with Russ Burgess (barely) and now I was back home getting ready to eat supper as soon as my father got home from work. Dad came in around 4:15 pm and wished me a happy birthday then sat in his "morris chair," that's what he called it. It was a heavy wood framed chair with a cushioned seat and back-rest that reclined partially, if so desired.

He then read the Herald News, you know, the newspaper that most likely tasted like Shredded Wheat, while I watched "The Amazing Adventures of Superman" starring George Reeves as the caped crusader or "The Life of Riley." I loved The Life of Riley and also "The Ozzie and Harriet Show" because they both had teenager boys in the show that were doing similar things to what my friends and I were doing…or at least we wanted to be doing.

I would like both shows even more in the next season, because "Junior" from The Life of Riley and "Ricky" (Nelson) from The Ozzie and Harriot Show both bought hot rods and I loved hot rods even at that young age. Ricky's car was a green '32 Ford roadster and Junior's car was, a '34 Ford coupe with a Chrysler "Hemi" engine. Both cars were very cool.

Anyway, in about 30 minutes supper was ready and Mom called us to the dinner table. After supper was over Mom or Dad, I can't remember which one, asked me to go into the kitchen and get a tray of home-made ice cream from the freezer. Mom said, for reasons unknown to me then, "Make sure you turn the light on so you don't trip." Trip, I thought, why would I trip? I knew where everything was. Anyway, I entered the kitchen and pulled on the over-head light cord and that's when I saw it. Sitting right there at the far end of the kitchen floor, near the door to the cellar, was a brand new Schwinn Green Hornet bicycle! "Holy crap!" Who's bike?" I yelled. Mom and Dad were standing there when I turned around and Dad said, "It's yours, happy birthday!" Then Mom said, "And please don't use the word crap."

I could not believe it was mine! What a beautiful bike this was. It was a 26 inch Green Hornet with horn case, front head-light and rear package carrier. Wow, I never, ever expected this! It was green and cream in color with white wall tires and it was the nicest bike I had ever seen! It was much nicer than Pussy-foot's Blue Panther.

I wanted to take it right out and go for a ride, but my father said that would have to wait until tomorrow as it was getting too dark already. "But, it has a head and tail-light" I argued. I gave up on that argument quickly without a verbal reply from him, he just gave me that look that father's had and that was enough. I asked if I could put it in the living room so I could look at it while I watched TV and he said that would be fine. I was so distracted by the Schwinn that I couldn't even enjoy The Gene Autry Show.

It wasn't until years later that I thought more about this gift and what it really meant. I figured that, at the time, my father made about $1.50 per hour. That worked out to $60.00 a week without any overtime and that amount was before taxes. Yet, he managed to scrape up the money to buy this bike for me, which, at the time, went for approximately $75.00! That was a pretty expensive present for the times; especially considering his wages.

Anyway the next morning I was up at the break of dawn. Usually the sound of my mother shoveling coal into the furnace and shaking the grates to drop the burned coal ash or "clinkers" to the bottom for removal would wake me up, but this day I was up before that, and ran downstairs just to look at my new bike.

My mother told me I would have to wait for my father to get up to take the bike outside. "Jezzz!," I thought, It seemed that all you did as a kid was wait for a grown-up to do something, never fully realizing that you weren't really up to too many of the tasks you thought you were up to.

However, after my father got up I finally got the bike outside and went for a ride. I rode it all day in the cold March air with Roy and several other friends. Roy had a maroon and cream colored J.C. Higgins with some sort of coil spring suspension up front. It was a great day of riding and the new Schwinn kept me from realizing how cold it really was. I felt like a million bucks riding this great new bike.

Then just before going home for supper, who comes riding up the street on his Schwinn Blue Panther? Yep...you guessed it...none other than the aforementioned *Pussy Foot!!* This was not good, and I started to get very nervous about what might take place!

Sure enough, he rides up and says, "Hey you little shit-head, where the f--k did you get that piece of shit bike?" The use of the "f" word by him added to the queasy feeling I already had in my stomach! I mean none of us used the "f" word…yet that is! I know that, because at the time, the worst word we used was "shit." I recall that with great retrospect due to an incident that occurred the previous year in Mrs. Woodhoff's class at the University of Delawanna (School #8).

My friend Ted wrote a note and passed it back to me, (he sat in the front of the classroom and I sat in the back). When I opened the note it said, "you shit"(I was not sure what that meant as no punctuation was included, so I'm not sure if it was a request, command or a question). Anyway, I wrote my own note back to Ted that read, "eat shit," (I included an exclamation point to avoid any confusion as to how it was meant). Well, Ted immediately raised his hand and Mrs. Woodhoff, said, "Yes, what is it Ted?" Ted then told her, "Bob just sent me this note" and handed it to her! Mrs. Woodhoff opened the note and I saw her eyebrows raise as she placed her left hand on her chest. She then looked towards me and said, "Robert!…come up here this instant!" When I reached her desk she said, "Where did you learn such a thing?" Then I showed her Ted's note to me. Up went her eyebrows for the second time in as many minutes and she exclaimed, "Teddy Tattersal!…what the"…she stopped herself in mid-sentence and said, "Both of you come with me right now, we are going to the principal's office!" Wow, we almost made her swear, I thought!

Boy was she ever mad! Mrs. Woodhoff was a very stern teacher, but she was also very fair. Many times she would catch us with items such as a "Wee-Gee" water pistol or a "Duncan" Yo-Yo in class and just confiscate it with no further repercussions, but this time she was very visibly upset and it looked like further action was going to be required.

Ted and I followed her to the Mr. Rosenfeld's (the principal) office. She explained to him what had just occurred and showed him both of our notes. Mr. Rosenfeld looked at them briefly, excused himself for a moment, and took the notes inside his office, closing the large oak door with the frosted, crisscrossed wire reinforced window behind him. Mrs. Woodhoff stood there with her arms folded across her chest looking at Ted and me while shaking her head. In a few minutes Mr. Rosenfeld came out and his face was as red as a beat. I thought, we are in big, big trouble now, he really must be mad! (It wasn't until years later that I realized he was probably laughing behind his closed door!)

Anyway, a parent/teacher conference was required and then our parents found out what we had done. My mother was astonished to learn that I had written that word and prodded me to tell her who I learned it from. I told her I learned it from Ted because she liked Ted and there most likely wouldn't be any restrictions placed on us because of that. I was right, she just told me how disappointed she was in Ted and me, which made me feel bad enough. I couldn't tell her I really learned it from Dean, a friend that lived behind me, because she was always a little concerned with my friendship with him and didn't really like his ways or trust him.

That little lie I told her was perhaps the start of a life-time of Ted getting blamed for things he didn't really do! Although it probably all evened out for him, because he didn't get caught at a lot of things that he really did do! None of which were really all that bad, but considering the time period I'm referring to, it seemed that everything we did was scrutinized to the ninth-degree!

We always thought we were in trouble for something. Sometimes we were; like the time a year or so later Ted and I, for some inexplicable reason, either got or put tar from a boat we were building and trying to seal onto Maryann Marcioni's new red coat! I can't recall if it was *got* or *put*. Two little three letter words, but a big difference in the culpability and punishment department here! As I think hard back to that day, I'm going to have to go with *put,* because even though it was so many years ago, my mind's eye will not let me wash away the memory of Maryann's mother walking up my drive-way with her fists clinched and, if it's possible for humans to have "steam" coming out of their ears, then she definitely had steam coming out of hers! (It sort of gave me a "cold icy, tingling feeling" that ran through my entire body. It was a feeling I wouldn't experience again until the first time I had to "slam" the brakes in my car to avoid an accident. You know…like when your eyes see something that your mind instantly translates into a possible life-ending situation! Boy, was she pissed! Gee, I wonder why?!

Back to my dreaded encounter with Pussy-Foot or "The Foot" as some of his friends called him. I personally, would be more comfortable calling him "The Foot" rather than Pussy Foot to avoid any tongue-tied screw-up in the pronunciation as I indicated previously. However, I don't think we were allowed to call him anything at all, not even Jimmy, his given name. But, that was Ok with us, because we really didn't want to be that close to him anyway, you know…anywhere within arms reach!

So after his initial un-friendly comment about my bike, he says, "Gimme that f--kn' piece-of-shit! "Who the f--k said you could have a bike like mine?!" "I'm going to smash the shit out of ugly green piece-of-shit!" I immediately jumped on my bike and took off for home with the "Foot" right behind me in hot pursuit screaming all kinds of obscenities at me. Well, I pedaled that Schwinn like I never pedaled anything before in my life. It was like a matter of life and death to me!

At the time of the encounter I was about four blocks from my home and I thought for sure he would catch me before I made it there, but he didn't! He never gained on me at all (probably because he smoked cigarettes). In fact, after two blocks I was opening the gap a little. He broke-off the chase about three houses from mine and yelled, "I'll get you someday you little bastard!" Maybe so, but not today, I thought!

Finally, the Cheerios or the crappy tasting (in my opinion) Shredded Wheat must have kicked in and good won out over evil; just like on The Lone Ranger Show! Man, this guy made Russ Burgess look like an alter boy!

Come to think of it, Russ really was an alter boy. At the time he attended St. Stevens Church on the corner of Delawanna and Linden Avenues. It also comes to mind that the local archery club used to meet in the basement of St. Stevens. Apparently that is where Russ learned to shoot the bow and arrow, albeit not with great accuracy.

When I got back home that day I asked my father to help me bring the bike back in the house. He said I should leave it in the garage out back instead so, I told him of the encounter I just had and that I was afraid of Pussy-Foot stealing it and destroying it. He said he would take care of that as he knew Mr. Rau, Pussy-Foot's father. It must have done some good, because it was my last problem-encounter with "The Foot." Although I never let my "Foot" guard down.

My relationship with Jimmy (Pussy-Foot) Rau changed as we grew older when were on the same ground in a maturity sense. We got along very well later in life. Actually, I found him to be a very nice and likeable guy. He's still pretty scary looking though, and years later when he owned a two-tone black and white '55 Pontiac Catalina, I made sure that when the time came for me to buy a car,

I didn't buy one that was similar to his in any way, shape, form or color to his, just to play it safe!

Another one of the "moderate or part-time," bullies was Dayton "Butch" VanHouten. Butch wasn't really all that much of a bully at all, in spite of having the name "Butch." Usually guys named Butch were almost always bullies, but he was sort of friendly most of the time. But, just like Russ, not all of the time.

Butch used to sell us younger kids turtles he caught down at the pond. He also always had a large supply of firecrackers he would sell to us during the summer months. He was quite the entrepreneur when he wasn't chasing us or making some sort of threatening gesture.

Actually he was one of the least feared of the older guys with bullying tendencies unless, that is, he was carrying his bow and arrow. Bow and arrows were prevalent in Delawanna in those days due to the large wooded areas and ample fields available to hunt in. However, the sight of a bow and arrow in the hands of some of these guys was seldom a welcomed one to say the least!

Butch was fond of making us stand in one spot and then shooting his field tipped arrows up into air where they would disappear from sight. He would then order us stand there until the arrows came back down, sometimes too close-by for comfort. I will say that he stood there fairly close to us and was also in risk of being struck, but he was enjoying it…we weren't! Thankfully we were never struck, (the Russ Burgess sneaker incident not withstanding!) It occurred to me that my friends and I probably faced more arrows being shot our way than The Lone Ranger ever did!

Butch got his pay-back several years later as he was driving to school in his Palisade Green 1950 Ford Tudor Sedan. Butch had been having tire problems at that time and as a result, he kept an ample supply of spare tires with him. Two of these spares were in the back seat during a particularly hot summer day. We all know what happens to air in a tire when it is exposed to heat; it expands. Well, one of the tires exploded while Butch was driving and it nearly blew his ear drums out. His ears were ringing for days! The headliner in the Ford was completely destroyed from the blast! He was lucky he didn't lose his hearing or worse. But, I guess that's still better than the prospects of having an arrow protruding from the top of your cranium!

Bullies were not confined to one age group or another, as evidenced by the Pavero twins, who were in my age group, but one year older than me. They looked innocent enough with their neatly groomed blonde hair and their always cleaned, pressed and up-to-date identical attire, which was always a step or two above what everyone else had to wear. They always looked sort of "dressed-up" if you know what I mean.

Now if they were by themselves, which was rarely the case, they were fine. But if they were together, which always seemed to be the case, and you happened to be alone, then they turned into instant bullies! It happened to me one day during summer vacation when I went down to the School #8 baseball field / school yard to see if any of the guys were there. Well, the only guys there were the Pavero twins. They were hanging out by the large Oak tree next to the flag pole adjacent to the ball field. I walked over and said hello as I knew them both and had one or both of them in my class at one time or another. The Pavero twins, for some odd reason, got left back in the same grade together! I guess it was a twin thing.

Anyway, it started off bad right from the get-go when one of them said, "What the f--k are you doing here?" "Did you come here to get your ass kicked?" I somewhat nervously told them that I just came to see if there was a ball game. The older one, Bill (he was supposedly three minutes older than his brother Gerard) said, "Oh yeah, there's a game, can't you see all the players out there on the field, shit-head?!" (This was the second time in recent days that I was referred to as "shit-head" and it always seemed to precipitate aggressive behavior against the person being called a shit-head.) I replied, "Well, see you guys later." I then started to walk away, but my escape was quickly blocked by Bill, who ran up in front of me and said, "Where the f--k are you going?" "I thought you wanted to play baseball!" I said, "I'll come back later" and tried to walk around him, but he pushed me back and Gerard jumped me from behind wrapping his forearm around my neck pulling me backwards. They wound up getting me on the ground and when they started throwing punches I decided to just focus on one just of them. I was able to get Gerard off of me and I pinned him to the ground. Bill kept punching me in my back and head and I kept punching Gerard while trying to fend off Bill's punches as best I could. Then, luck of the Irish, I saw my buddy Joe Mattiello running towards me. Joe pulled Bill off of me and now the odds were even (not something the Pavero twins cared for). Neither Joe nor I were very aggressive and were not inclined to fight unless a situation like this arose, but on this day we gave the Pavero twins their long-deserved, old-fashioned ass-whuppin'! Now, not only did they look identical and wear identical clothing, but now they both had identical bloody noses! Even though I wound up with a few lumps myself, it was worth it to see them get theirs, thanks to Joe's great timing.

Finally, chalk one up for Shredded Wheat and Cheerios! Actually, maybe it was the chicken catchatori Joe's Mom use to make for us! Or possibly it was the home-made wine his Dad used to let us sample after we helped him with the "recipe"! As they say, "a glass a day keeps the doctor away" or was that an apple a day?

Either way, one or all of those things helped us kick the Pavero twin's asses that day and, I'll have to say, it felt pretty good!

The Pavero twins eventually wound up on the other side of the bullying one day on our way home from Woodrow Wilson Junior High School and while on board bus number two. On this day some of the kids were smoking in the back of the bus. This went against the school and bus company policies without saying. Anyway, the Pavero twins went up an advised the bus driver of the illegal smoking that was going on in the rear of the bus. The bus driver immediately pulled the Public Service Bus Co. bus to the curb of Brighton Road and Glen Oaks Court, walked to the rear of the bus and proceeded to confiscate all of our bus tickets, there-by eliminating the benefit of riding the bus to and from school until this matter was resolved by the school principal.

Once the bus was under-way again Bernard, a.k.a. Buddy / B.B. Hudson, who lived near the twins and was sick of their crap, decided it was time for a tutoring lesson in come-up-ins for the look-a-like little squealers. Buddy was a pretty big kid, but he had a very laid-back and friendly demeanor…normally that is! Today, however, was a different story!

The problem the Pavero twins had was that while everyone else grew in physical size, they seemed to stay the same and lost their physical advantage even thought there were two of them. But their reputation was that they were bullies and no one forgot that! Now even worse, they were "tattle-tales"!

Buddy asked a couple of us to get the twins and bring them to his seat in the back of the bus where he always sat right in the middle of the rear seat facing the aisle. I was eager to oblige due to many negative encounters with these two bullies turned titwillows. So along with, I think, Joe Mattiello, and with assistance from most of the kids in the front of the bus who blocked the drivers rear-view mirror view, we grabbed the Pavero's from their seat and escorted (dragged) them to the rear of the bus for a consultation with newly appointed tutoring head-master in ass-kickin', Buddy Hudson!

All things considered, Buddy took it pretty easy on them as they both pleaded for mercy. He gave them both a little "tune-up" (identical, as I recall) and sent them back to their seats. They never really bothered anyone from that point on.

Chapter Three:
Inertia Can Be a Bad Thing.

These encounters with the older guys, although somewhat intimidating, and at times dangerous, were still not as bad, to us, as the dreaded "depantsing" I referred to in "Hot Rods, Pink-bellies and Hank Ballard," from a humiliation stand-point, that is. To a boy growing up in that era, being stripped of your clothing was the ultimate in shame. The danger of the bow and arrows, if given the choice, would have been much preferred to the embarrassment of being depantsed. Especially depending on the degree of the depantsing!

If you were lucky, they only removed your trousers and hoisted them up the flag pole at the end of Dunney Park. Most of the time you could hide in the bushes and wait for a friend to come by and retrieve them for you as the flag pole was located at the far end of the park in plain view of Delawanna Ave. If you were not so lucky, they would remove all of your clothing and possibly take them with them! The term "depantsing" didn't mean they would only remove your trousers. There were no rules to this mortifying ordeal except that it was randomly played whenever the whim struck them. They (the older guys) were always the "depantsers" and we were always the "depantsees." There was no fate worse than being left completely naked running for the bushes with your tally-whacker out for the entire world to see, especially if it was covered with Calamine Lotion!

This type of torture would not work on the kids today as they willingly wear their pants half way off in the name of style! But, back then, the thought of being depantsed left us trembling with the anticipated humiliation of it all! I mean, kids had songs they would sing to embarrass you if they even caught a glimpse of your underwear, ie; I see London, I see France...you know the rest.

Depantsing was probably some form of sub-conscious primal behavior that, fortunately, our group didn't inherit when we reached the age of the older guys. We had no desire to remove some boys clothing. We were too busy trying to figure out how to perform that same deed on the girls our own age, which proved to be, in most cases, a futile effort. Maybe that's why the older guys resorted to it! Fortunately we chose hot rods as a diversion.

Back to my new Schwinn Green Hornet. I eventually felt it was safe enough to leave my bike in the "shop" behind my house adjacent to the garage. The "shop" was actually an old blacksmith's shop that was on our property and was the size of a large one car garage. It also had a loft which became my friend's and my clubhouse. There was a grape barbour directly in front of the shop and a huge cherry tree next to that. These both provided a lot of shade. I would clean and polish that Schwinn there and make whatever adjustments need to be done in the coolness that the shade provided.

One of the first things I did to modify the Green Hornet was to go down to the lampshade factory across the street from School #8, of which my friends and I were all students at the time. There I picked scrap pieces of hard cardboard or flexible fiberglass from the garbage to be used for creating the sound of a internal combustion engine by fastening the material to the front fork with a clothes-pin so it would protrude into the spoke area of the front wheel. Hence, when the wheel turned and the spokes would hit the cardboard or fiberglass material, it would emit a popping sound that would increase with the speed of the bike, sounding, to our ears, like a motorcycle.

Most kids used baseball cards and even balloons to try to duplicate the sound of a gas engine. Balloons sounded the best, but did not have a long life and would pop after limited pedaling. This type of behavior displayed by us boys was rather odd to the girls as they required none of this to enjoy cycling.

I also added some custom accessories such as the chrome support rods / handle-bar braces that attached to your handle bars and bolted to the front wheel axle. These chrome plated rods were adorned with several red, blue and green reflectors and were all the rage back in that time period. Next I added a fringed pleather (looked like leather, but was some sort of vinyl / plastic) "Hopalong Cassidy" tool bag that hung from the rear of the seat and two reflector laden mud-flaps; one on the front fender and one on the rear fender. Another addition was the use of various name brand soda bottle caps pressed between the front and rear wheel spokes. Very cool I thought, all the while hoping that the "Foot" didn't have any of these same accessories! He probably used beer bottle caps in his spokes anyway.

The Green Hornet was kept in very good condition for a couple of years until the car-bug started biting harder. I then started modifying it to satisfy my fledgling hot rod desires as it would be a number of frustrating years before I would have an actual car of my own.

One of the first modifications was to remove all non-essential parts such as; the front and rear fenders, chain guard and horn tank, you know, all the stuff that originally made the bike so cool. It had to be stripped down like a hot rod for speed! Then I actually added a car steering wheel to my handlebars! How crazy was that?! But, I was not alone as most of the other guys did the same thing. What I didn't realize was that not having a chain guard or fenders proved to be a dangerous thing as I soon discovered.

One night Ronnie Kohn, John Wilson (a.k.a. Poncho) and I decided to follow Clifton Fire Department Engine Four's Ward La France fire engine while it was en-route to a call. We were pedaling as fast as we could down Oak St. trying to keep the fire engine in sight when, just in front of School # 8 (Delawanna University), my dungarees got caught in the sprocket causing the chain to come off! This created a situation of not having anyway to activate the "New Departure" rear coaster brake! (we used to argue which brake was better; New Departure or Bendix.) The answer is; *neither*, when your chain comes off! That, coupled with the fact that these Schwinns had no front brake meant that I was now traveling as fast as I could on a down-hill grade with no brakes at all!

To complicate matters, we were heading towards a dangerous ninety-degree turn at the bottom of this grade just in front of Rivelli's Tavern. I knew I would not be able to make it around that turn at this speed, so, fortunately, or unfortunately, I decided to slow the bike down by pressing my foot against the front tire. At first it didn't seem to help, so I applied more pressure which caused my foot to ride up the tire and jam into the front fork.

Well, this definitely did the job of stopping the front tire from turning, but inertia had a different effect on the rest of the still speeding stripped-down Schwinn Green Hornet hot rod. The conflict between stopped front wheel and still moving rest-of-the-bicycle caused the bike to flip from the rear and "pole-vault" me through the air crashing me face-first onto the paved road surface below me!

According to eye-witnesses, (the story is never good when it starts with; "according to eye-witnesses") I passed Ronnie in mid-air and, after hitting the ground I slide across the road-surface for approximately twenty feet. It knocked the wind out of me and I thought I was going to die! Ronnie and Poncho dragged me to the lawn of School #8, where, after a few minutes, I was able to breathe in a somewhat normal fashion again. . My face and arms looked like the surface of a well-done pizza pie. My legs were in a lot of pain from hitting the steering wheel/handlebar as I was catapulted over the bike. The automotive hose clamps I used to secure the steering wheel really cut up my legs pretty bad. This, I guess, was the price I had to pay for trying to be cool!

Anyway, Ronnie and Poncho helped me get home. They then went back to retrieve the old Green Hornet hot rod, which also suffered it's share of road-rash. After several days of recuperation, I was as good as new, well almost . See, like I said before, I needed no one else's help in getting injured!

Unfortunately, this incident would not be my last experience with involuntary flight from a bicycle. On Easter Sunday the following year several of us; including Poncho, Phil and myself met at Dunney Park after church. We were all still in our dress clothes from attending mass when we decided to go to DeCamp Bus Lines garage over on Main Ave. and buy a soda from the Canada Dry machine they had near the passenger waiting room. Well, we all hopped on Poncho's 24 inch Schwinn with me pedaling, Poncho sitting side saddle on the frame directly in front of me and Phil sitting on the handle bars with his feet supported by the front wheel axle stubs. The position of Phil's feet would play an important role in what was to happen next.

As I pedaled on the paved walk-way, which was on a slight downward grade in the direction we were traveling, we picked up speed as I stood up to get more force into the pedaling. Then, without warning, the bike up-ended and cart-wheeled, throwing us to the pavement! Phil got the worst of it because he was sitting on the handle bars and was slammed into the asphalt walk-way face-first!

When the dust cleared, I saw Phil all scraped-up with the knees ripped out of his new dress pants. He was sitting there with no shoes on! Then I saw his brand new John's Bargain Stores loafers on the ground with the tops torn half-way off! As it turned out, Phil inadvertently turned his feet inward and they got caught in the spokes causing this latest two-wheeled calamity. All three of us had cuts, bruises and ripped clothing. Phil was banged-up the worst, but his main concern was for the shoes, which his mother recently bought for him especially for Easter Sunday Mass! Hard to go home and show your Mom shoes like these with any kind of reasonable explanation.

These incidents helped us to understand the effects of inertia from a first hand basis, but they were much more painful than learning from a text book!

Another day, completely ignoring the fact that I had this recent rash of incidents, I offered to ride Mickey Pastula down the embankment of School # 8's baseball field and over, what we called the "double-bump." It was quite a sensation to hit this double-bump at *speed* (there's that "S" word again that would from time-to-time play a negative role in a lot of our activities). Going over the bump gave you that "butterflies-in-your-stomach" feeling and we would do it for hours at a time. But I had never ridden with someone on my bike while going over it, and thinking back now, it probably wasn't a good idea to take as my first passenger, someone nicknamed "Porky"!

However, not thinking past the end of my nose, Porky (Mickey)and I jumped on the bike and *started* down the hill with him sitting sideways on the main frame bar. I say started, because we never finished. About half-way down I slammed on the pedal operated New Departure coaster brake to add some flare and excitement. This action accomplished exactly what I had planned, except the flare and excitement was only for the on-lookers and was at our expense, actually at my expense. The bike slid out from under me and the right side pedal dug hard into my right inner calf! The added weight of my waist-line challenged buddy was pushing the pedal harder into the injured leg.

We were not able to get untangled from this mess until the audience stopped laughing enough to help. Mickey had a few minor cuts and I had an odd looking bruise that hurt like hell on my inner right calf.

I didn't dare tell my parents of this latest bike incident because I thought they would take the bike away for sure. After several days the injury looked much worse and the pain increased. After a week or so I had a purple lump the size of a hard ball on my leg. Finally my mother noticed it and took me to the doctor. The doctor lanced it and squeezed out the coagulated blood admonishing me for not telling someone as I could have had a blood clot travel through to my heart or lost my leg from infection! *Yikes!* Not good! I thought, I have to start being more careful, three crashes in a very short period of time. They say bad things come in three's. Well they're wrong! As I would prove in the next week or so.

Jimmy Walsh (nicknamed ; "Fatty," great!…another weight challenged riding partner to up the injury quotient substantially) and I decided it would be a good idea (nothing we thought of was really ever a good idea!) to remove my front wheel and slide my front fork axle slots over his bike's rear wheel axle studs and fasten it in place, there-by creating a bicycle-built for two! Oh we created a bicycle-built for two alright; two idiots!

We never considered the fact that the bikes would now articulate in the middle and bicycles built for two did not! We also never gave a thought to the fact that the front fork had several degrees of inclination built into it which would have an adverse effect on the articulation geometry, unintended as it was. This experiment was an accident waiting to happen! And happen it did, and when we reached our first turn!

Fortunately for me, it was now someone else's turn to endure the consequences of one of our bright ideas. This time Jimmy took the brunt of the pain as I was able to jump off this geometrically challenged train-wreck with only a slight sprained ankle before all the effects inertia, centrifugal force, gravity and geometry took affect! (We weren't doing very well in the bicycle riding department, but we were sure starting to learn a lot about science and math!) Jimmy actually didn't fare too badly either, all things considered. So, I ran (limped) home and fetched my front wheel from which we made we made two bikes from one again! These bike incidents seemed to be coming more frequently, albeit, self induced.

Another "hazardous to your health two-wheeled activity" every boy with a bike used to partake in was to ride through the noxious fog of pesticides created by the city's mosquito spray machine!

The City of Clifton used to pull a mosquito fogging machine around behind a red World War Two Army surplus Jeep. They mainly covered the areas of the city where the mosquitoes were most prevalent; that included Delawanna due to the large ponds, swamps and wooded areas.

When they pulled this machine around a thick, white cloud of sweet smelling pesticides would roll out of the back of the machine and we would ride our bikes in and out of this, unbeknown to us at the time, poisonous mist! The operators never said anything to us, so we would follow them all over town. In later years it became evident to us that the pesticide they were using was D.D.T! Great!...just wonder-freakin'-full! This might have accounted for the high ratio of boys repeating grades in Delawanna at the time. This was another activity engaged in by the boys only. No wonder the girls always seemed to breeze right through school. They were smarter to start with! The girls rarely took part in any of these hair-brained, risky pastimes. Most of them that is, but not Sandy. Sandy is a friend and neighbor that you will read about later.

The girls did everything different than the boys back then. They even had separate entrances into school from the boys with the words ("Girls" and "Boys") very legibly inscribed in the concrete arch over the top of both entrance doors off School # 8, and any other school I have ever see that was built in that same era.

They didn't even want the girls walking through the same entrance as us! Why? Who knows, I guess they didn't want the girls getting any of "*us*" on them! (In a biblical sense that is!) Whatever the reason, it sure seemed to work better than any of the ideas they have come up with today in regards to raising kids, which don't seem to work very well at all! Can you imagine if boys and girls were made to use separate entrances today! Wow, major lawsuit here! Also protests, picket lines, naïve, brain-washed, ultra-liberal parents screaming into television cameras about fairness, equality and discrimination! You can take me back to the fifties anytime now!

Thankfully though, Roy and I always donned our U.S. Army regulation gas masks purchased at Curry's Army and Navy Store while riding through this poisonous cloud of gas. Not for any reason other than we thought...where the hell else were we going to use them?! Hopefully it minimized the loss of some brain cells caused by inhaling D.D.T.

So far all of our off-spring have the correct amount of body parts with no extra ears or thumbs growing from their foreheads! We did repeat some grades though! D.D.T. or A.D.D.? Who knows...maybe a combination of both.

Back in those days everyone knew there was a difference between boys and girls. We even had separate entrances to the "University of Delawanna" (Public School # 8) as shown. They didn't want the boys anywhere near the girls if they could help it. This would not fly today with all the liberals and the A.C.L.U.'s interference in life the way it was...and should still be!

Chapter Four:
Baseball Diversion

At times I wondered if I would survive intact to actually be able to get my automobile drivers license with all these two-wheeled misadventures I was having, so I decided to divert myself into something less dangerous. Not that riding a bike in itself was considered dangerous; it just was the way that my friends and I rode them that made them dangerous.

Anyway, I decided to try-out for the new Little League division that had recently been started in Delawanna. Back then they actually had try-outs. You had to make the team or they sent you home rejected with a psychological disorder that could, by today's way of thinking, make you a serial killer!

So, Saturday morning try-outs at Dunney Park came and I showed up with Roy, Tommy Walsh, Ted Tattersal, George Gray (Swissy) and just about every other boy from Delawanna between the ages of nine and twelve. The coaches and managers of the newly formed Delawanna Division lined us up according to ages and threw balls for us to field and pitched balls for us to hit. It became apparent very early in the try-out process who the better players were. They then started ranking us by skill levels and placing us in different sections of the field. I quickly noticed that I wasn't in the same section as Tommy and Ted. Tommy was probably the best all-around player among us. He had a very hard-to-hit curve ball, even at that age. Ted was also a very good ball player and could throw the ball well.

I could see the way the groups were being set up that the best players were on one side of the field and the worst players were at the other side of the field. Tommy, Ted and Roy were together with the better group and I was in the middle between the best and the worst. That was fine with me because it looked as though I was at least going to make a team. My fielding was so-so, I could hit the ball though; I had to, because I couldn't run very fast, or as the coach was fond of saying, I ran doubles into singles!

Anyway, after all the groups were categorized, which included a "farm team" (the farm team category meant that they were prolonging any psychological damage to the child for the time-being) The kids that didn't make it at all were sent home to a life of misery, ridicule and destructive behavior like setting cats on fire and later to be subjects of F.B.I. profiler studies!

After this process the managers started stacking, I mean picking the teams, of which there would be five: St. Clares, Givaudan, Relock Fence, Bobker Bearing and P.T.A. P.T.A.?! What the hell?!

Well, naturally of all the teams to be on, no one wanted to be on PTA! After all PTA stood for Parents Teachers Association. What boy wanted to be on a team that conjured up any image that had anything to do with school? *Double Yuks with an Oak Leaf Cluster* on that. It did appear to me that the best players seemed to be on St. Clares roster. Why? I don't know. Papal influence possibly?

The rest of the players were placed on the four other teams in a graduating downward skill level based on what the managers and coaches could ascertain from what they had seen during try-outs. After St. Clares made all their picks; Tommy, Ted and Roy made it on St. Clares, they then filled all positions on Givaudan and Swissy got one of them. Then the Realock Fence and Bobker Bearing team rosters were filled. It was at that time that I realized, because I had not been placed yet, that I was going to be on P.T.A.! *Oh Holy Crapola!* Hey, at least I wasn't on the "farm team" or worse yet…sent home with the future serial killers of America!

It was now Mr. Lowry's turn to draft players for his team, P.T.A. Not that it was a secret or anything, as all of the kids that were left knew we were going to be on P.T.A! Well, Mr. Lowry grabbed his clip board and called my name first. Well, at least I'm one of the first losers, I thought. He then continues to call out the rest of the names of the kids that will be on the dreaded P.T.A. team.

Tom, Ted, Roy and Swissy (he actually wasn't known as Swissy this early in our lives) start saying things like, "Wow P.T.A., do you think you'll have to attend their meetings?" Wonder what logo the uniforms will have on them? Maybe an apple…" Ha, ha…yeah, yeah…how about you guys eat the bird," was my response to that. Then I said, "At least I'll have less of a chance of getting left-back," when all the while I realized getting picked on P.T.A. was, in itself, like getting left-back, at least in my mind.

Well, after all the humiliation I headed home and my father said to me, "So, did you get on Joe Lowry's team?" I said, "Yeah, how did you know?" He then proceeded to tell me; "Joe and I have known each other since we were kids, so I told him to see what he could do to get you on his team."

"What?," I said, "You mean to tell me that is why I'm on his team?" Dad says, "Yep, pretty good huh?" I said, "Dad, do you know what team he is in charge of?" He said, "No, not really." I said, "It's P.T.A.!" "Do you know what P.T.A. stands for?" He says,"Ah…I don't know…maybe Pacific Transit Authority or something like that?" I then told him what it stood for and he just said, "Hmm, sorry, but that's not so bad. Do the shirts actually say Parents Teacher Association or do they just say P.T.A." I said, "I don't know yet but, either way it makes it feel like I'm playing for the teachers!"

The following Wednesday as I got ready to go to the park for practice Dad handed me a bag and when I looked inside I found a brand new Rawlings Mickey Mantle signature outfielders glove! Wow, this is cool, I thought. It made me forget the P.T.A. thing for a while, but not for long.

After several practices it was decided that I would be the catcher. Hmm, not bad, I thought. Pretty neat actually, although I didn't know where my new glove would fit into this position, but it was starting to sound better to me.

At the last practice they gave us the uniforms. I quickly looked at the blue and white shirt and on it were the initials, P.T.A. Well, not as bad as I thought. At least it wasn't spelled out for the world to see.

Well, our first game was against; you guessed it…St. Clares! *Crapa-freekin'-roni!* I have to play against Tom, Ted and Roy. Tom pitched for St. Clares and almost no one could hit off him. He was unbelievably good for that age and had a great curve ball.

I got quite a workout as the catcher though, because our pitcher was the complete opposite of Tom, and everyone hit off him! He was unbelievably bad for that age! My workout came not from catching balls, but from trying to stem the constant flow of St. Clares players from coming across home plate. Now I know why he chose me as the catcher. I was really more of a goalie than a catcher! A catcher is supposed to catch things, like baseballs! However, very few baseballs made it past the St. Clares batters to my glove! Most of them were hit, no, make that smashed into the outfield, where they were then thrown back and forth between all the fielders while the base runners ran at me like I kicked their mother! Any balls that did come back to home plate from the fielders would have required the use of a step ladder or a Lacrosse net to retrieve! Well, thankfully they didn't have electric score boards back then with the score up in lights for the world to see!

After several more miserable outings like this I actually started defending the plate like a goalie! One particular kid on Givaudan (Skip) used to always taunt the pitcher and me by running half-way down the base-line and back. He was always trying to steal home to add insult to injury. Then he would smirk at us whenever he was successful. It got to the point where I didn't just want to tag him out, I wanted to knock him out!

He did this time after time and almost always got away with it, because I usually never had a ball in my possession to tag him out with; except one time when he tried to steal on a ball that got past the pitcher. This time as he ran from third to home the second base-man, for some odd reason, actually picked up the ball and threw it to me! Imagine that!

The throw was a little high and to my left, so I had to jump as high as I could, which was not very high believe me. But, I caught the ball and came down right on top of Skip effectively ending his baseball stealing career for the rest of that season! It was the highlight of my season! Good thing, because highlights were few and far between while playing for P.T.A., unless of course you call having the parents and the teachers sitting in the stands rooting for you a highlight, which I didn't! Yeah, that was just great! Like being associated with the teachers wasn't bad enough, they actually had, at times, come to some of the games to cheer us on! I would rather have had a route canal; maybe even get depantsed…eh…on second thought cancel that depantsing thought !

My baseball career lasted up to the point when school let out for summer vacation. Then there were far too many distractions for me to concentrate on playing, especially when the only way we didn't lose was by the other team forfeiting the game or a rain-out. That, along with the fact that whenever the manager's son felt like he wanted to wear the catcher's equipment I would be made to play first base, which I hated. It was hard to play at any other position after being a catcher, because I became so accustomed to wearing all the protective equipment that I felt almost naked out there without it. Also, the manager's son couldn't catch a ball if they walked up and placed it in his glove, so whenever he caught, the score that we generally got beaten by, increased significantly! He usually caught for only one inning, or until he got bowled-over by a runner. And that was most likely to happen as we could have used a cop to direct the flow of traffic from third plate to home plate!

One day, during one of his son's whims, the manager ordered me to first base again, but this time I couldn't get my mind off going fishing down at the Old Pond with Al Beyer. We had gone fishing earlier in the day and he was going to go back after supper, but I had to play ball, which I was rapidly losing interest in. So, instead of taking my position at first base the next inning, I just went home and got my fishing pole to join Al at the pond; just that simple…never giving it a second thought! It must have been nice to be that care-free back then.

When my father went to the park that evening on his way home from work to watch me play, he asked Joe Lowry, the manager, where I was. The manager was, at that point, unaware that I had left until one of the other kids told him and my father that I went fishing, there-by effectively ending my baseball career. The good news was, fishing was great and the bad news was, the chance now existed for another encounter with Russ Burgess and his bow and arrow!

Chapter Five:
Waterlogged Shotguns and Disappearing Wallets

Now that the summer was here, I had lots of extra time on my hands, especially since I didn't have to play baseball anymore. Most of my extra time was spent down at the Old Pond and surrounding woods during the day and then Dunney Park or one of the other hang-outs at night where we would watch the antics of the older guys, most of whom now had their drivers licenses.

Often the older guys, one of them being my cousin Eddie, would venture down to the pond/woods down behind School #8 with their girlfriends. At that time my friends and I wondered why in the world they would want to bring their girlfriends to the woods! How could they go fishing or hunting with girls tagging along? Wouldn't they just get in the way? Especially dressed the way they were with saddle shoes and white sox and their hair all made-up and all. Plus, we thought, why would they want to come down here with the girls when they had cars they could work on?! Didn't make much sense to us…at the time. The real reason was lost on us then. Boy, the innocence of youth!

Within a few short years though we would be praising them for actually being able to talk the girls into going to the woods with them! It never worked for us though! The girls we hung-out with would say, "Go to the woods with you guys? "Sure, why not? You guys go now...and we'll meet you there later. If we don't make it you can start whatever it is you had in mind without us!"

Anyway, back to the pond. One particular day my cousin Eddie, Lenny Loman, (aka, Mack), Ronnie Meyers and a couple other older guys, all who were members of "The Bishops" (a local club, of which there were several based on age groups) and some of their girlfriends came down to the pond while I was there fishing with a couple of friends.

As we stood there talking, numerous small splashes appeared in the water just in front of us and something hit the leaves of the trees to our left, immediately followed by a loud bang. When we looked around we saw two kids standing in the woods across the pond at the banks of the upper ("New Pond") looking towards us. At first we didn't realize what had happened, but then we saw one the kids raise his arms and we saw a puff of smoke followed by the splashes in the water again and then a loud bang. My cousin said, "Those bastards are shooting at us!" It turns out they had a shotgun and they were actually shooting it towards us!

Eddie said, "Follow me, and walk slowly back up the hill like we don't realize what they are doing." When we got to the school yard Eddie said, "Lets go around the pond by the trail where they can't see us." So we walked around the pond hidden by the trees and then walked west on the Rt. 3 (called S-3 back then) shoulder until we came to the New Pond (the man-made pond just above the Old Pond, proper name; Yantacaw Pond).

We then walked down the eastern most trail alongside the pond and came up behind the two kids catching them by surprise. The older guys grabbed these kids and slapped them round a bit, which was nothing compared to what they could have or maybe should have done to them for actually shooting at us!

The gun, which turned out to be a twelve gauge shotgun, was in a case and in the hands of one of the kids when we got there. These kids were around sixteen years of age and said they came from Nutley, the next town over and to the south of Clifton. Mack took the shotgun from them, pulled it from the case and found it to be still loaded with several rounds of # 4 shot. It was a good thing the smaller shot lost it's effectiveness before it reached us or someone would have been seriously injured or worse. It might have been a different outcome to the story if they were using buckshot!

These kids were now crying and pleading with Eddie and Mack not to hurt them. They kept saying they were sorry and that the shotgun belonged to the father of one of them. "Sorry?," Mack said, "You're sorry because you got caught you little shit-birds!"

Mack then fired all the rounds left in the pump operated Savage shotgun into the woods and then motioned as if he was going to throw the gun into the pond. The kid whose father owned the gun, pleaded with Mack not to do it because he said his father would kill him if he found out he took the gun in the first place!

Not being too sympathetic to the kid's cries, Mack made good on his threat and threw the gun as far out into the water of the New Pond as he could. Then he grabbed the kid and said "You want it?...go get it!" then he pushed the kid into the pond. Eddie grabbed the other kid and said, "Go help your friend" and pushed him in also. They both climbed out crying like babies with the older guys calling them "pussies," "titwillows" and other derogatory and insulting names. They told them if they ever saw them back here again they would throw them in the "chemical pond." The chemical pond was a small pond behind The Berkshire Chemical Co. where the drain-off from the plant emptied into! It was the pond that one of our friends, Johnny Hilt, ventured into one day on a dare and came out looking like Peter Pan! It was always a different color, but on the day Johnnie went in, it happened to be green, so, after he emerged, Johnnie was also green!) Johnny had a stuttering speech impediment that was pronounced when he was nervous or excited. When he got out of the pond, he noticed his change of hue and clamored, "Wha, wha, wha what ha, ha, happened? We stood there laughing our asses off asking him where Tinker Bell was!

Anyhow, back to the pond incident, we left the two kids standing there soaking wet and crying and anticipating the punishment they faced when they got home.

All things considered, they got off pretty easy. I'm not sure if they were ever able to retrieve the gun, but I doubt it as it was thrown quite a distance from the shore-line and out into the deeper water.

Maybe Russ with his bow and arrow wasn't so bad after-all. At least Russ didn't intentionally shoot me, or at least I don't think he did! I started to think maybe I should reconsider this baseball thing after this latest episode.

Normally after supper my friends and I would meet at Dunney Park or at the Suburban Market on Delawanna Ave. After we all got together we would play some kind of a game like; Spaniola, Five-Ten-Ringalario or Kick the Can.

Spaniola started out with one, two or more guys that were "it." The guys that were "it" had to bend over and all the other guys, the guys that were not "it" would jump over their backs one at a time using one of the many torturous and humiliating ways or "calls" the lead jumper would call out, such as; "Eagle Claws" where the jumper would dig his finger nails into the backs of the guys that were "it" as he jumped over them, followed by all the other jumpers doing the same thing! Sort of a sadistic version of "leap-frog"!

One of the calls was "Pull the old ladies underwear." This

required every jumper to grab the "it" guys underwear and pull them out of the back of their pants and then let them go, there-by snapping them against their backs. Now that doesn't sound too bad, does it? And usually it wasn't, unless of course Russ Burgess was playing!

One day Russ was a jumper during a "pull the old ladies underwear" call and grabbed hold of the "it" guy's underwear. The "it" guy in this instance, thankfully for me anyway, was Rich Lamon. Rich was a strange sort of guy and always looked unkempt. His hair was almost always disheveled; it sort of looked like he combed it with a rock!

Well, Russ pulled his underwear and kept pulling, actually swinging Rich around by his underwear waist band until he ripped almost all of his underwear right out of his pants! Russ took one look at them then held them up for everyone to see and said, *"Eeeeyyuuukkk, I guess you didn't take a brown check this morning!!"* This sight brought the warning to mind that your mother always gave you. You know the one when she said, "Never leave home without clean underwear on!"

Rich spent the rest of the day trying to convince us he had been sick, but no one was having any of it! Unfortunately for Rich, a very undesirable new nick-name was born for him that day; Especially when we found out he still had his pajama bottoms on under his jeans! From that day forward he was known as; "Skidz," as in "skid marks in your underwear"! I think if you get a name like that, it's time to relocate as your "attractiveness to girls meter" just dropped to zero! Kind of hard to rebuild your image after that; especially when you didn't have much of an image to start with!

"Kick the Can" was really our favorite game to play when it got dark. Kick the Can was sort of a hide-and-seek type game where one team of guys were "it" and the other team were the "hiders." The object was to find the "hiders" just by visually recognizing them; they didn't have to be tagged or anything like that. Once caught, you would be placed in a "prison" and then the it guys would go back out to look for the rest of the "hiders." The problem is that anyone of the guys on the loose (hiders) could come back to the prison and kick the can that was left there to guard the prisoners. Kicking the can away now allowed the prisoners to escape. This was provided they weren't seen by the guys that were "it."

We used to set-up agreed upon boundaries before hand. But, there was always the chance that after you counted to one-hundred to allow the hiders to scatter, they might just go home leaving you out there looking for them until you finally realized what they did! You could be out there looking all over for them and they might be home watching "The Untouchables" on TV! This happened on occasion, but not that often.

We even invented a game of our own we called "the wallet trick." It was simple; We would tie fishing line to an old wallet with monopoly money sticking out of it, place the wallet in the street, run the line across the sidewalk (held down by a rock) then hide at the top of Ronnie Kohn's steps to wait for a "victim."

It was unbelievable how people would stop their cars over the wallet and actually dive under the car as we pulled the wallet away! Some would actually start chasing the moving wallet!

Tom Hand, an elderly, gregarious, black gentleman that lived near-by, chased it half-way up the steps before he realized what was happening! When he saw what we were doing, he laughed so hard I thought he would bust a gut. He laughed all the way back to his car saying, "Man, you got me, you got me good!" He was a good-natured guy and a good sport about us "getting over on him," but not everyone was. Some people, out of embarrassment I guess, would break the wallet from the line, take it from us and curse us out.

This all came to a screeching halt one day when Ronnie, Tom, Poncho and myself were playing the wallet trick and a Clifton cop stopped for the wallet. As he bent over to pick it up, we pulled it away from him! Well, when he saw us, he ran after us, and ironically caught Tom, who was by far the fastest runner of us all! We all came back to face the music and were just given a stern lecture for our escapade. This incident, though, ended our wallet trick for good. Too bad, it was a boat-load of fun!

These days, when we all get together we reminisce about things like this. The last time we did, Tom Walsh tried to talk us into doing the wallet trick again! You know…now that I think of it…nah, we better not!

Chapter Six:
Underage Driving and a Caboose on the Loose!

Dean was the first one of the guys in my age group to buy his own car. We were thirteen or fourteen years old at the time and the car was a '51 Ford convertible that he bought for $50.00 from one of the older guys, Mike Passafume.

Dean and his older brother, Tommy, lived in a large two family home on Main Ave. in Delawanna, adjacent to Dunney Park. It was on a very large piece of property, I would say at least an acre and a half. It was owned by a guy we called "Charlie the Fishman." Most of the property was overgrown with reeds and swamp-like growth due, in part to, a spring from the "Third River" running near-by and under the rear of the property.

Anyway, Dean talked Charlie the Fishman into paying us to clean up the property and then using the driveway and surrounding land for his car, once he got all the money to purchase it, that is. Dean and I worked on cleaning up the property for about a week and when we were through it looked twice the size with the reeds and under-growth gone.

After we were paid for our efforts, Dean had accumulated

enough money to pay for the Ford, which he did and Mike delivered it the very next day. Mike gave Dean many warnings about driving on the street without a license and the consequences that would follow if he ever did. At the time, Dean agreed with all of the warnings.

Dean and I spent a good part of that day washing and waxing the Mexicali Maroon convertible with the dented right rear quarter panel. The car ran very well and we took turns driving it around the now cleared property. Dean's brother Tommy and Charlie the Fishman also gave stern warnings of what the consequences would be from them if we ever ventured out onto the road with the car. We assured them that that would not happen. I knew there was no-way I was going to do that. It seemed to me to be an irrevocable criminal act only committed by "juvenile delinquents." What I didn't know at the time, was that Dean did not have that same idea.

We did have a lot of fun with the car for several weeks driving it around the oblong track we created with the radio turned up until the speaker distorted. It was during that time that I first noticed the effects music had on our mood and behavior. When we heard "Problems" or "Bird Dog" by the Everly Brothers we felt like spinning the tires and sliding the car around the turns in our, somewhat, confined driving space. When they played "One Summer Night" by the Daneliers or some other slow ballad, we slowed down and cruised wishing the girls were with us. We took turns driving the car and it was quite a thrill for us at the age of thirteen and fourteen. We would drive that old Ford all day and all night! I couldn't wait to eat my supper and get back to Dean's house and that old Ford.

We drove around our little track at night with the top down listening to Jocko Henderson's show called; "Jocko's Rocketship," "The Ace from Outerspace." We waited for Jocko to play Ricky

Nelson's "Poor Little Fool" or Conway Twitty's "It's Only Make Believe" and those songs left memories that I still re-live whenever I hear them. It occurred to me way back then that music is a very powerful stimulant! A good old up-tempo song still makes me feel like burning the tires off my hot rod to this day, some fifty years later!

One time Dean did a wheel spinning start as I was trying to get in the car and as I grabbed the vent window post to pull the door shut I crushed the fingers of my right hand between the vent window post and the windshield pillar! The door actually latched…ouch! That ended any fun for me for a day or two. Jeez, I can still feel the throbbing pain in my finger tips when I think about it!

Well, the day finally came when Dean could no longer resist the temptation of driving on the road. He took a set of plates off one of Charlie's old Ford panel truck's that was no longer being used and put them on the '51. I told him that I wasn't going and I thought he was crazy. But, that didn't stop him and he hopped in the '51 with two new kids that recently started hanging around: Al Berg and some kid named Poncie. I didn't care for either one of them. Things didn't feel the same from the day they started coming around. Both of these guys were always ready to do something I was uncomfortable with, and so was Dean, for that matter. I realized that Dean always had the propensity to go a step-over-the-line and now he had two new friends with a similar mind-set. These guys came from Passaic and Dean met them there on one of his trips trying to steal records at the Lincoln Music Shop on Lexington Ave.

The three of them took off down Main Ave. and I went home. I really never went back to Dean's house again after that. It was definitely the point where we drifted apart. On occasion I would see him riding around in the Ford. Sometime he would stop and say,

"Come on, don't be a chicken, you can drive!" I never took Dean up on the offer. Dean's brother eventually found out about him driving on the streets and made him sell the Ford just as he threatened he would! That didn't stop Dean's desire to drive illegally though, or his new uncontrollable wanderlust. One time Dean, Al Berg and a local girl by the name of Eileen Batsio stole a delivery truck from the Thomas Bread garage on Cherry Street and headed to the southern states!

They made it as far as Delaware when they were caught! I mean, how much more obvious could they have been than driving a Thomas Bread step van!? I guess it could have been worse. They could have stolen the Oscar Meyer Wienermobile!

Dean's life at that point definitely started heading in the wrong direction and after several more encounters with the law, he was sent to "Jamesburg" one of the youth correctional facilities in South Jersey. He eventually learned from his early misguidance and straightened his act out later on in life.

It certainly was a distraction; the yearning to drive thing all us teenage boys were going through at the time, but even though some of us might have eventually taken a quick, albeit illegal ride on the street, none of my other friends ever went to the degree that Dean would go.

The Thomas Bread garage that Dean stole the truck from was a maintenance shop as well as a depot for the delivery trucks and on staff were two full-time mechanics. Both of these guys were in their forties at the time. John, a pudgy little guy, that resembled Lou Costello, owned a '54 Ford Customline tudor hardtop, it had a Cadet Blue roof and a Dove Gray body. It was a V/8 with a standard three-speed stick-shift transmission. Eddie, the other mechanic owned a Tuxedo Black '56 Mercury Montery tudor hardtop with red, black and white interior.

Jimmy Walsh (no relation to Tommy)and I used to hang out at the Thomas Bread garage on a regular basis during the summer and watch John and Eddie repair the trucks. We also used to hound them to let us wash and wax their cars for some extra money. Actually the term "extra money" would indicate that we had some money already that we were trying to add to. But that wasn't the case. The fact was we had no money at all and were trying to think of ways to earn some money.

After some convincing, they both agreed to let us clean and detail their cars. What was very surprising though was that after they asked us where we intended to do the work, which we was going to be Jimmy's yard on Delawanna Ave., they flipped us the keys and just let us take the cars, even knowing that we were underage! That reaction from two adults seemed, in our minds anyway, to legitimize our driving these cars on the street, even though we were underage. I guess they figured Jimmy only lived a couple of blocks away, how much trouble could we get into. Thankfully, we didn't have any problems. What a thrill it was to drive those cars even if only for a couple of blocks. They could have easily talked us into waxing them for free!

Hanging with Jimmy didn't necessarily guarantee that you wouldn't get into some kind of trouble; like the time he de-railed a caboose! He didn't do it intentionally, the derailment that is, but he was screwing around with a siding switch and left it in the partially thrown position, which caused the caboose to de-rail! Jimmy stayed home for several days afterward, until the heat died down from that episode!

One of the guys took a wooden box full of signal bombs from the disabled caboose and it seemed as though every boy in Delawanna had a supply of them after that. These were small explosive devices that train conductors would strap onto the rail to notify the next train crew how far ahead of them the train that last departed was. They would explode from the weight of the train and were much louder than an "M-80" or "cherry bomb." At times you would hear ten or fifteen go off as the kids that had them would strap them to the track, never considering the danger it presented to the trains.

Another Jimmy incident occurred one day when Jimmy, Ronnie and I were hitch-hiking from Passaic back to Delawanna. Jimmy's next door neighbor, Mrs. Boyle, stopped to pick us up in her 1952 Buick four door sedan. Ronnie climbed in first, then me and finally Jimmy got in, or, I should say Jimmy attempted to get in. Anyway, as soon as Jimmy was partially in the car and as he reached for the door to close it, Mrs. Boyle accelerated pretty hard and Jimmy fell out of the car onto the roadway right in front of the Montauk Theater. I looked back and saw him sitting on his ass in the middle of Main Ave. waving for us to stop! After we notified Mrs. Boyle of her lost passenger she stopped and picked him up pretty much unscathed, all things considered. That was a typical Jimmy Walsh incident of which there were many!

Jimmy's house was a cool place to hang out at due to his sister Joan's fiancé, Oakly Blake. Now Oakly was a very nice guy and used to pay a lot of attention to us kids whenever he came to Jimmy's house. But, an added bonus to us was when Oakly's brother, Donnie came around.

Donnie was an accomplished and respected automobile customizer and belonged to a local, highly recognized hot rod club called "The Drivin' Deuces." As a result, when ever Donnie and his friends came by we would see custom cars; some that were well-known and featured in the rod and custom books of the era. It was quite a thrill for us younger guys to know these fellows at the time. Still is!

Chapter Seven:
One Last Belt for the Road and the Speed-Shift King

Watching the older guys became a daily ritual for us as we hit our middle teenage years. They were a source of information and entertainment and we would live our lives vicariously through them hoping for the day when we would be able to drive...legally. The lure of freedom that cars would provide excited us, but watching these guys was all we could do for the present time.

One of these guys, Ronnie Meyer's, had a '48 Ford with a bad rod bearing knock. When he dropped the pan to inspect it he found the crankshaft was in very poor condition and to repair it properly would require removing the engine and giving it a complete rebuild. The word, properly, seemed to get in the way more often than not when it came to repairs such as this. All these guys wanted to do was get back on the road as quickly as possible. That's just what happened when Ronnie pondered this needed repair and it also helped him make a decision to get rid of the car and get rid of it...now! The problem was he now he had a car that was apart and not drivable and if he put it back together, it still would have a very noticeable rod knock.

To rectify this current situation Ronnie got an old belt, you know…the kind of belt you hold your pants up with, cut off a piece, soaked it in oil, then wrapped it around the crankshaft journal and replaced the rod bearing cap! He started the engine and to everyone's amazement, it sounded great! So, he immediately drove it down to Pete Sadowitz's Auto Wreckers and Fine Used Car Sales on River Road and traded the Ford plus a small amount of cash for a 1948 Plymouth coupe!

Now, I didn't use this learning experience as a repair guide, but I now knew to look at the oil pan to see if it had recently been removed. It didn't bother Ronnie to scam old Pete, because he said Pete screwed so many people that he should have called his business; "Pete Sadowitz's Auto Wreckers and Brothel"!

We ran into Ronnie quite often due to him and his family, including his older brother Bobby, living upstairs in my buddy Joe Mattiello's house on William Street, the same street I lived on.

Both brothers were into cars and they always had something interesting around for us to drool over. I remember the day Bobby Meyers was selling a '32 Ford three window coupe. The car was somewhat apart and had no engine, transmission or interior. I knew enough about cars to realize the car had been channeled over the frame rails and the top was chopped about four inches or so.

Anyway the guy comes to pick it up, and I heard Bobby tell the guy that he would take $35.00 for the car. I thought that was a fortune at the time and couldn't believe the guy was going to pay that much for this car that was in need of such serious help, as far as I could see through my inexperienced eyes anyway. I remember the guy looking at Joe and me upon seeing the look on our faces and then stating to us, "Someday you'll understand"! Boy was he ever right! And it didn't take too long either!

Another one of the older guys, Jack Jorgs, owned a '51 Chevy with a Buick engine. At the time, we were duly impressed with this creation and thought it had to be the fastest thing around, partly because he told us it was. He called it the "Chevick." It was a Belair Tudor Hardtop model and it was painted a dark metallic blue; G.M. called it "Trophy Blue" with a "Thistle Gray" roof. We never really saw it go or heard of any races that Jack had with the car at that time, but it had to be fast…right? I mean it had a 322 cubic inch, 195 horse power '54 Buick Century motor and, unfortunately, a Dyna-flow (or Dyna-wontcha-flow as we used to call them) transmission where there originally resided a little 235 cubic inch, 105 horse power six cylinder with a power glide (slush-box) automatic transmission.

Jack used to come over to Paul's Friendly Service Mobile Gas Station over on Main Ave. on a fairly regular basis. He had quite a reputation for driving, but as I recall, it seemed to be self-generated, as it was never corroborated by anyone else other than Jack! . At the time, circa ; 1960, many of us younger guys would hang-out at the station and get in Paul's way. We tried to help out and sometimes we actually did…I think anyway. It was hard to tell by Paul's reactions, because the ever-present cigar clamped between his teeth masked any discernible facial changes. Both favorable and unfavorable reactions had the same shake of his head to one side as he turned to walk away! It was a reaction I would see from Paul many times in the years to come. In time I was able to figure out the good ones from the bad ones though. Paul let us hang-out at the gas station because we were all friends with his daughter, Paula. I guess he figured the more time we spent there with him, the less time he had to worry about us spending time with Paula; a well-meaning father's concept I figured out later on in life!

Back to Jack's Chevick and his self-described driving prowess. One day while at Paul's, Jack was holding class with those of us in attendance on the positive outcome of races due to the effects of his expertise in "speed-shifting." Jimmy Walsh had just gotten his driver's license and recently bought a V/8 stick-shift '51 Ford two-door sedan with a very faded Glen Mist Green factory paint job. Jack was, at this point, verbally instructing Jimmy in the art of speed-shifting and how important it was to be as proficient at it as he, Jack, of course was. My thoughts at the time centered around the fact that Jack's car was not stick-shift, but had an automatic transmission. Not just any automatic transmission, but a Dyna-flow! Probably the worst choice in transmissions for any application other than possibly driving a bunch of blue-haired old ladies to church in your massive G.M. sculpture of sheet metal and chrome with a transmission that gave the impression of starting off in high gear and staying there! It seemed to me that a guy who was extolling the virtues of speed-shifting in such an enthusiastic manner, would, at the very least...own a stick-shift car himself!

At any rate, his verbal and animated explanations and expressions reached a point where he said to Jimmy, "Let's go for a ride in your car and I'll give you your first lesson in speed-shifting." With that Jimmy flipped Jack the keys and climbed in the passenger side of his '51 Ford, allowing Jack the wheel so as to continue with this in-depth lesson on speed-shifting that was about to now conclude with a real-life demonstration.

Jack fired up the Ford and the dual glass-pacs made a nice deep, mellow sound. This would be the last "mellow" sound to emit from the old Ford for a while, but not the last "deep" sound! (Blown transmissions do have a deep sound to them...don't they?)

It seemed very deep to all of us observers as we witnessed Jack rev up the old "8BA" 239 cubic inch flathead and then pop the clutch leaving Paul's lot with the rear wheels spinning, throwing gravel and cinders all over the gas pump island! Then came the perceived, long-awaited and expertly executed speed-shift to second gear...*Ca Clang, glang, glang, glang...g-a-a-a-laaang!* Hmmm...very deep sound there, but now missing the mellow part, I thought as we watched the Ford roll to the side of the road and into DeCamp Bus Lines parking lot!

As I looked back, I saw Paul walking away and notice the familiar head shake to one side! Sort of looked like it fell in the unfavorable category to me.

Jimmy's old Ford was towed back to Paul's with Jack telling Jimmy there must have been something wrong with the shift linkage, because that never happened to him before. How could it, I thought, he doesn't even own a stick shift car!

The lesson I learned from all of this was to not let Jack Jorg drive my car whenever I got one! Unless, of course, it had a Dyna-flow transmission...which it wouldn't!

Shortly after this incident I finally got a ride in Jack's Chevick. He asked Billy Walsh, Jimmy's brother, and I if we wanted to take a ride to Suffern N.Y. as he needed to pick up a carburetor from some guy. We quickly accepted and jumped into the Chevick......Suffern was about ¾ of an hour to our north (long ride for a carburetor, I thought) and it was all highway from Clifton to Suffern. During the ride there and back Jack "got on" the Chevy several times there-by blowing the myth/image of this car, at least for me, as being the fastest car around. I didn't know what car was, but it was definitely not this car! It had to be the Dyna-flow transmission that hindered the performance of this car, putting it into the category of just another "blue-hair taxi," albeit a nice-looking one.

I guess it was just as well it wasn't stick shift, at least that lessened the percentages of him blowing the transmission with another speed-shifting exhibit and leaving us stranded in New York State!

Chapter Eight:
Hitch-Hike Nightmare, Pool Table Benedictions and an Extra Large Can of Whoop-ass Please!

Thoughts of cars were now starting to take an almost overwhelming part of our concentration and we would do anything to hang-out near the older guys that were already driving. However, they barely noticed we were there and we almost never got a ride in their cars. Maybe if they saw us hitch-hiking they would pick us up, but that was about it.

We did a lot of hitch-hiking in those days and even had hitch-hike races. We would split into two teams starting out on the intersection of Main and Delawanna Aves. We would then start hitching in opposite directions. One team would hitch to Passaic and the other to Nutley and then back to the starting point. First team back won! Won?…won what? There was no prize! We certainly had no money to wager! I don't know, maybe we just felt getting back safely without being kidnapped was winning!

We would then discuss the types of cars we got rides in. If you were really lucky, some kid would pick you up in a hot rod or custom car. That was always the best, unless of course you were picked up by Larry Komar from Passaic (the next town over) as Roy and

Poncho did one night. We all recognized Larry as he recently started coming to Delawanna trying to woo the girls, but we didn't know too much else about him. Anyway, during one of our hitch-hike races he stopped his 1950 Oldsmobile 88 Two-door Hardtop and asked Roy and Poncho where they were headed. They replied "Down-town Passaic." He told them to "hop in" and they started heading north on Main Ave. towards Passaic. As he approached the crest of the hill near the border of Passaic and Delawanna and just before reaching the downhill side about 1/4 mile from Passaic, Larry informed Roy and Poncho that he was going to commit suicide! And…he was going to do it "now"! He then slammed the gas pedal to the floor fully opening the throttle on the 303 cubic inch over-head valve Olds Rocket V/8 engine and started on the downhill side of the hill aiming the Olds at the D.L.L.&R. railroad bridge abutment near the Passaic border! Wow!…shit luck for Roy and Poncho for sure! And to think I was jealous that they got to ride in this cool looking Olds!

The car was a mild custom with a silver gray bottom and a black roof. It was nosed, decked and had white wall tires that were mounted on red painted wheels where the red paint could just be seen at the edges, as the rest of the wheel was covered by spun-aluminum "Moon Discs"! Very cool, we thought…at the time! It was a car any kid would die for and, unfortunately, at the present time it looked as though Roy and Poncho might just do that!

However, none of the Olds' allure mattered anymore…at least not to Roy and Poncho as they headed towards this concrete wall at high speed with Passaic's very own "village idiot behind the wheel"! Larry was not just an ordinary village idiot, but a suicidal village idiot!

Funny how things are when I think of how, at the very same moment that Ronnie and I were so envious of Roy and Poncho wishing it was us that got a ride in Larry's car; Roy and Poncho were screaming at the top of their lungs in fear for their very lives; pleading with this "nut-case" to "please stop"!

In a final last-ditch effort Roy grabbed Larry by the throat and threatened to kill him if he didn't stop! Then, in a move that made no sense, he, thankfully, stopped the car! I thought, why did that stop him? His intention was to kill himself and he stopped because someone threatened to kill him??? Who knows why, but the final out-come for Roy and Poncho was all that really mattered. They exited the Olds and walked back rather than risk another ride with Larry. That incident put a hold on our hitch-hike races for a while!

This would not be our final contact with Mr. Komar though, as you will see later on in this book.

Winter time was the worst time for us as the older guys didn't come around as much and there was really not that much for us to do. At times we would go to the hall in the rear of St. Clares Church whenever they had teen night. There we would play pool and dance with the girls, etc.

On one winter Sunday morning at around 11:00pm Ronnie Kohn, Poncho, and I decided to see if the rectory hall was open. Much to our surprise it was! So we went in, made ourselves at home and decided to play a game of pool. We racked up the balls and someone broke them, all the while never giving consideration that there was probably a mass going on just beyond the removable partitions directly behind the alter and only thirty-five feet from where we were playing pool!

Well, within a minute of the breaking of the pool balls and the accompanying cracking sound of the ivory balls banging into one another, Father Dempsey came through one of the doors leading from the alter, and boy did he ever look pissed! It was sort of hard to tell with him though, as he always looked pissed to us anyway. He reminded us a lot of Pussyfoot and could have easily passed for his father, both in looks and meanness along with the whole connecting eyebrow thing.

Well, he was so mad that he started screaming at us using so many expletives that he was the one that needed to go to confession afterwards! Man, that was one pissed off Irish Man-of-the-cloth! I never heard a priest swear before, but this guy knew more bad words than we did and I'm sure the whole congregation heard him as well! Fortunately, he wouldn't be able to see our faces when we went to confession or we would have had to say Hail Mary's and Act of Contrition's for penance for the rest of our lives!

Father Dempsey would have really been pissed if he knew that on our way there we stopped by DeCamp Bus Lines and went over to the Canada Dry soda machine; you know the type that had all the bottles slid into rails that required you to put your coin in to unlock a hinged locking devise that allowed the bottle to be extracted. Well, at the time, we thought it was funny to open the lid, pop off the soda bottle caps and drink the soda through a straw leaving the empty bottle in the rack. We thought it was funny that is, until we got caught and were made to sweep out the waiting rooms and bathrooms to pay for our crime. It was a lesson well-learned.

He wasn't as pissed off as Bruce, one of the older guys was, when another one of the older guys (Yonko) plastered bumper stickers all over his '58 Plymouth Plaza Sedan the next Spring. Yonko didn't put them on the bumpers, he put them all over the Misty Green factory paint for reasons unknown to me other than just going too far with "ball-busting"…way too far!

On the evening in question Bruce left the Plymouth down at Dunney Park and went somewhere with one of the other guys; a common practice among the older guys.

Yonko, who was one of the guys that used to hang-out with the older guys on a daily basis, decided to plaster Bruce's car with bumper stickers! Someone said to him, "Bruce is going to be pissed off when he sees what you did"! Yonko's short reply was, "Oh yeah, well f—k him!" Hmm, this sounds like a fight coming for sure. Both of these guys were pretty well built, with Yonko being the bigger of the two. However, they both looked like they could handle themselves.

Bruce was the quieter of the two, and Yonko was a much more vocal character. Neither one of them ever gave us younger guys any trouble at all, so I had no real favorite if a fight ensued other than I thought what Yonko did was pretty bad and if anyone needed to get an ass-kicking it was him. All the older guys though, had their money on Yonko as the most likely victor should it come down to a fight.

Within about an hour Fred Schroeder's black and white '56 Ford Customline pulled up the curb adjacent to the park and four or five guys exited the vehicle. One of them was Bruce and as he walked toward where everyone else was gathered he noticed the stickers all over his Plymouth. He looked over the car for a minute or two and I could now see the rage building in his face! He then walked up to the group standing there, of which I was one, with his eyes on fire and his fists clinched and said in an extremely agitated voice, "Who is the piece-of-shit-scum-bag that did that to my car?!" No one said anything at all, but most of the guys, who wanted no part of Bruce at the present time, looked towards Yonko. Bruce walked over to Yonko and asked, "Did you do that to my car?," to which Yonko replied, "What if I did?" Bruce then said, "If you did, your going to take them off and pay for any damages, that's what!" Yonko said, "Eat me, dip-shit!"…and then it started!

These two guys fought from the park and out onto the street, slugging it out! It was the first fight I ever witnessed with the older guys and they fought hard! Bruce, eventually beat-the-living-crap out of Yonko! Something the other guys never thought would happen.

Yonko got up off the ground after the fight, got in his white 1960 Pontiac and drove away without saying a word. He never, ever came back to Dunney Park again, or anywhere else for that matter. I guess he couldn't face the guys after getting his ass kicked; Especially since he started the fight in the first place! Just because a person might seem to be a push-over, doesn't always mean they are! Bruce definitely must have eaten his Shredded Wheat that day!

No one else ever tried screwing with Bruce after that! The guys, including Bruce, never talked about the incident again, but we did, because it was the first time we ever saw anyone fight like that before!

Chapter Nine:
I Feel Faint

One day things got a bit boring for us down at Dunney Park. The older guys were out for a ride, it was too early to play "Kick the Can" and not enough of us to play "Spaniola" or one of the other games we played, so we decided to try "fainting" one another! That's right...fainting!

We had only recently heard about it from a guy by the name of George Cheechi. Some of us went to school with him and he would come to Dunney park on occasion as he only lived a few blocks away. He fell somewhere in between our age and the older guys. He was sort of in a no-mans land all by himself in age groups and he really didn't completely fit in with either of the groups as he had an odd, self-centered sort of personality. He wasn't driving yet, so he didn't fit in with the older guys and the only way he fit in with us was, even though he was two to three years older than us, he was in the same grade as most of us from having been "left-back" several times. He was also one of the guys that was "sent home" from baseball try-outs! Uh-oh, possibly a serial killer was in our midst! He was always sort of grumpy and constantly spitting, which certainly didn't endear him to the girls our age.

His nick name was "Chogie." I'm not sure how he got that name, but it was probably because his body was shaped like cigar! He kind of tapered down at both ends and was a bit stout in the middle! Actually if you put the plump side of two pares together, that would be more representative of his body shape! But, I guess Chogie was a lot easier and more fitting of a nickname. Otherwise we would have had to call him "Two-Pares"! Too confusing for outsiders and it sounds too much like a Native American Indian's name. Mmmm, How...Georgie Two-Pares, you wannum playum faint game? Nah...Chogi was a much better choice for sure! Plus in all the TV Westerns I'd seen, he didn't look anything like an American Indian who all seemed to be lean, solid and muscular. Chogie was none of these; he was fat, loose and flabby. In fact, if anything, he looked a lot like the previously mentioned "Jingles," you know...Wild Bill Hickock's side-kick! He resembled Jingles in appearance only and that's where the similarities ended. Jingles was a gregarious, jovial and helpful sort of fellow and Chogie scored double-zeros in all of those categories.

At any rate, I made up my mind when I first laid eyes on him that there was no-way I was getting on any bicycles with this fat bastard any time too soon! Nope...I had already suffered enough injury multiplications from riding with lard-asses!

Anyway, Chogie tells us of a fainting game where you take a deep breath and then let all the air out, then someone squeezes you from behind and it is supposed to make you faint. Great, just what I wanted to do...faint down at the park! What then...do you get de-pants or something? Not the best idea we've ever heard, but there really was nothing else to do, so the consensus was, let's give it a whirl. It was my intention right from the start not to be a faintee, possibly a fainter, but definitely not a faintee.

After some discussion, Chogie agreed to be the first faintee. The problem was finding someone with arms long enough to wrap around Jackie Gleason Junior here! Joe Wilson, Poncho's brother, offered himself up to be Chogie's fainter and stepped up for a trial fit. Sure enough, Joe's arms could reach around our roly-poly walking watermelon of a friend here, so he was designated to be the first fainter. Wow…what an honor!

Ok, game on! Chogie takes the last few drags on his Pall Mall cigarette. I thought to myself, if he takes any more drags on that cigarette, along with the extra weight on his fat-ass, he won't require someone to faint him, he will faint all by himself!

Well, Chogie gets himself in a standing position and tells Joe to get behind him and wrap his arms around his upper mid-section, you know…in around the area the brand-name band would go if he was really a cigar. Joe complies and now Chogie says, "Now when I exhale, you squeeze as hard as you can and don't stop until I faint!"

With that the Chogmeister takes three or four deep breaths, exhales and tells Joe to "Faint me now!" Joe obliges and put all he had into it. All of a sudden Chogie sort of went limp in Joe's arms. Now Joe was a pretty strong guy, but nothing prepared him for this sudden and overwhelming pull of gravity generated by this now passed-out Harbor Seal sized person he was trying to hold up! Joe ultimately just wasn't up to the task and had to let go!

Well, "Mr. faint me now" falls to the ground to the sound of a tree limb snapping! He then snaps out of his self-induced mini-coma and starts screaming, "Ooohhh, my leg! I think my leg is broken, owwww!" With that everyone ran away! Our first instinct was always to run away, because we always thought we were in trouble weather we were or not; most of the time we were, somewhat; Especially Joe, because quite often he was in real trouble! Nothing really bad mind you, just dumb, mischievous things. A bit more dumb and mischievous than the rest of us. Like the time he stole / borrowed a cement tub from the construction site adjacent to the Old Pond and used it for a boat. One day he played hooky and paddled a cement tub out to the middle of the Old Pond…during school hours no less!

He was easily seen from the upstairs classrooms of School #8 by a teacher who informed the Principal, whom at that time was Mr. Robinson, to Joe's extra curricular activity. Mr. Robinson went to the top of the hill just above the pond and called to Joe while waving him to come towards him. Joe's second mistake was waving back to Mr. Robinson using only his middle finger! The article in the Herald News started with "Rub-a-dub-dub a boy in a tub!" Joe made all the necessary apologies and was made to stay after school for one whole month for the offense.

Back to our now very alert, conscious (I have to say, I liked him better in an unconscious state) and wounded, expert "faint-me" demonstrator, the afore-mentioned Mr. Chogie.

From the other side of the park we could hear Chogie screaming bloody-blue-murder, so some of us went back to check on him. Not Joe though, Joe was "grabbin' hat" as we used to say. After all he was the fainter and thought it was surely his fault, which, this time it wasn't. When we arrived back by Chogie it was easy for even us to see he had a broken leg! That's what happens when the weight of your body falls onto your leg and in this case it was the weight of at least two normal sized bodies testing the strength of this Pall Mall poster child's femur!

After getting his parents to come to pick him up and take him to the hospital, it was determined that he had incurred a compound fracture! Hmm, I now saw clearly how it worked, twice the weight, twice the fracture! Similar to my experiences in incidents with "porker" friends!

After he was released from the hospital he used to come down the park in a wheel chair and ask us to push him around all day, giving orders like; "take me here," "take me there," "get me cigarettes," "I'm hungry"…Ahh shut the hell up ya fat bastard!

This got old pretty quick. After a while when we would see him coming, we all got the urge to faint ourselves. It didn't help matters that he was more than a bit of a pain-in-the-ass, aside from his already grumpy demeanor. Otherwise we wouldn't have minded pushing him around, even with the added luggage he carried as a bona-fide fat-ass.

After a couple of weeks of playing "driving Miss Daisy"…wheel chair style, we would all "grab-hat" when we saw him coming! That was the end of the "fainting game," and, to our relief, Chogie sightings for a while. It was fun while it lasted…as long as you weren't Chogie!

After he got his drivers license, Chogie started coming around again and used to ask us if we wanted to go for a ride. The first time we did, he asked us all for twenty cents a piece for gas and an extra nickel if we wanted the radio on! I mean, no one had any objections to helping pay for gas, but the nickel for the radio seemed a little excessive! . Chogie had very short arms and very deep pockets as the saying goes. So, he was always asking to "borrow" money from us, which now led to us fleeing the park whenever we saw his car coming. We always had plenty of time to escape because he drove his Surf and Woodland Green '53 Chevy tudor sedan *soooo slooooow* to conserve on fuel. We could see him back out of his driveway four blocks from the park, giving us ample time to vacate the area!

At times we would be fooled as he would drive up, undetected, in his mother's Pewter Gray and silver '58 Dodge Custom Sierra station wagon.

We certainly didn't want to go for a ride in that thing for two reasons; there was nothing less cool to us than a big four-door station wagon and with the gas mileage this thing would get, he would want to charge us double!

He used to tell us he was going to go try to pick up some girls. Then he would point to the chrome plated glove-box and say, "I keep this highly polished, if I pick up a girl with a skirt, it acts like a mirror! You know…like a shoe mirror!"

Wow!…What a smooth operator! There was definitely no life guard on duty in the gene pool the day this guy was conceived!

Chapter Ten:
Five Quarts of Oil and Two Full Shovels of Sand Please!

Some of us kids started going over to Delawanna Building Supply across the rail-road tracks from Ronnie's house whenever the free-lance mechanic, George, was there to work on the equipment on weekends. We knew when he was there because he drove a '47 Ford woody wagon that was in very dilapidated condition.

This thing looked like it had a major-league termite infestation as almost all of the wood was rotted. Some of the doors were held shut with rope and baling wire! I would like to describe the color of this vehicle, but that would be almost impossible as almost all of the body panels were from another car and were all different colors. But, by using the parts of the cowl and "A" pillar that weren't primed or covered in tree sap, and using a forensic's point of view, I would have to say the wagon was originally Ford Midland Maroon. But knowing George, it might have been that the left front fender was the only original part of the car and in that case the car would have originally been Ford Strata Blue.

The left side rear window of George's car was plastered with stickers from numerous different states the car supposedly had traveled through during it's, obvious hard life. I'm sure this window must have also came from a donor car or perhaps it was the only original part left and that is why the car was in such poor condition. Although after getting to know George, we all realized why it was in the condition it was in. It was that way because it was George's car!

The front bumper was made from a four by six piece of unfinished oak. The dash board was missing most of the gauges and his key switch consisted of two wires that had to be twisted together to complete the ignition circuit! George had his wife's name "Blossum" painted on the driver's door. We never saw her, but we imagined what she looked like from the flattened out front passenger seat with the broken back cushion frame! We wondered, was she always named Blossum, or did he name her that after she gained all the weight that caused the seat frame failure?!

During this time we had only recently been allowed back to Delawanna Building Supply as a result of some of us being caught driving the company trucks around the yard one weekend…on the starter motors!! This idiotic act left several of the vehicles sitting in various places through-out the yard with dead batteries! Joe, the owner of Delawanna Building Supply, told Ronnie's mother about it and said he thought it was Ronnie and some of his friends that did it. After being questioned, we admitted to it and subsequently went over to apologize to Joe. We also offered to wash and wax several of his red and white Ford flat-bed sheet rock delivery trucks to make amends. Joe took us up on the offer and we learned a valuable lesson, both in humility and forgiveness!

Anyway, George would show up there early Saturday mornings in this piece of drift wood on wheels and about six or seven of his nine kids, (that all looked to be around the same age) would jump out of any door that wasn't wired shut and immediately start running around the yard in all different directions while George started calling out their names to no avail! He quickly gave up on corralling his look-a-like little munchkins and would just walk away and start whatever project he was there to work on. What a way to start a workday!

George would fix (make that work on) trucks, forklifts, cars etc. No job seemed too big for him to attempt (attempt being the operative word here). We would, in our youthful innocence, watch him all day trying to learn whatever we could. It took us a while to see it, but eventually we figured out that, although George was a very nice guy, he was not the best mechanic in the world. Actually if the Society of Automotive Engineers ever found out about George they would have probably amputated his hands so he could never pick up a wrench again!

He was always breaking bolts off, smashing his fingers, knocking things over and misplacing parts and tools. Nothing he did ever seemed to progress smoothly, with the possible exception of fathering numerous off-spring; all of whom seemed to be born deaf, as they never even looked his way when he called their names! At times during the day several of them would be seen running past the shop and surrounding areas. George seemed very unconcerned. He definitely was a very laid-back guy.

One time we helped George put a clutch in a forklift truck. When we were finished and as he was about to leave for home, he threw us the keys to the forklift and said, "Here, have some fun with it." We thought he was kidding, but he wasn't! As he pulled away, he leaned out the diver's window of his termite smorgasborgmobile and said, "Try not to kill yourself!" That was the extent of his instructions to us....just, try not to kill yourself!

Well, we drove that little Clark Clipper all over the yard and somehow avoided tipping it over, but I'm not sure how! We had it up on two wheels a few times though! I'm sure Joe, the owner of the company, would have been mortified with George's care-free offer to us kids!

One of the jobs Ronnie and I watched from start to finish was when George removed, rebuilt and re-installed the six cylinder engine in Joe's Dusk Pearl and India Ivory '57 Chevy Belair four door sedan. When he first attempted to start the engine, it wouldn't turn over. George stated, "It's a little tight because it's new." (No, it was a little tight because George rebuilt it!) He then hooked up another battery in series with the one in the car and now it turned over, but agonizingly slow. George added another battery, then another! Eventually he had 48 volts hooked up to the Chevy six cylinder just to get it to turn fast enough for it to even try to start. The valve cover and air cleaner were off during this fiasco and he kept, for whatever reason, resetting the valves during these attempts at starting the engine. He also kept dumping gas down the carburetor. Several times during these attempts it actually sounded as though it was going to start. Then, on the last attempt, it backfired and the gas he had just dumped in the carburetor blew back out all over the top of the engine…on fire!

George casually looked around for a fire extinguisher, of which there was none. He didn't feel the need to have one standing by being the care-free type of guy he was. George still had this unconcerned look on his face, but Joe didn't! As a matter-of-fact Joe was extremely stressed out to say the least! After-all he not only envisioned losing his car, but perhaps his building too!

After his almost futile search for something to put out the fire with, George finally found an extinguishing agent…*SAND!* That's right, sand! George walked over to a sand pile along side of the shop, grabbed a shovel and threw two full shovels full of sand right on top of the engine that was sitting there with no valve cover or air cleaner on it! With the fire finally extinguished, George said to Joe, "Ah, no big deal, don't worry about it. It will be fine."

Even we knew this was not the best thing for an engine and it probably wasn't going to be fine! Ronnie looked at me and said, "Yeah, my father always adds a shovel full of sand to his engine after an oil change!" I said to Ronnie, "Imagine how many more batteries he's going to need to turn it over now !"

Well old care-free George just went back to work like nothing ever happened! George never seemed to get stressed at all. That's because George was a stress "carrier"! Meaning, George gave stress to the people in his midst as evidenced by Joe who was now sitting on a railroad tie sweating profusely while holding his forehead and loosening his necktie as he probably felt like he was being strangled! I know the word "strangle" surely must have crossed Joe's mind as he looked in George's direction!

This experience taught me that you can learn something from everyone; From some people you learn how to correctly do things, and from some people you learn how not to do things! Old George seemed to always fall into the latter category.

All things considered, George's care-free personality probably added years to his life. That is, if he didn't set himself on fire!

Chapter Eleven:

Blue Berry Facial and Van the "Ripper"

The yearn to drive was burning inside all of us boys. Most of the girls never even mentioned driving or cars, except for Sandra Ward, the girl I mentioned earlier. Sandra lived two doors away from me on William Street and we were friends since we were little kids. She used to threaten all the older guys that already drove that when she got her car they had better be ready for her!

I was not sure what she meant by that, because it looked like her first car, at least the one promised to her, was a 1950 Plymouth! Not very intimidating in the horse power department to say the least, but she was not one to sit back and just let the guys spout off about what they had or what they were going to get without putting in her two-cents.

This female bravado that Sandy, at times would display, used to get under the skin of one of the older guys, Tommy Farrel. He was always telling her to "Shut the hell up and beat it or he would kick her in the ass!" She in-turn would tell him, "Hey Sonny Boy, if you feel frogish, why don't you leap?!" Whew!...that really used to piss him off! Sometimes he would chase after her, but he never could catch her!

One night while everyone was hanging out at The Suburban Market Tommy showed us all a box full of blueberry preserves that he got from a guy named "Stretch" who worked at the Dairy Queen on River Road. I don't remember what Stretch's given name was, but he supposedly played drums on The Shirelle's first hit record, "I met Him on a Sunday," at least that's way the story went. Most likely true, because he did play the drums, and The Shirelles were from Passaic, the next town over from Clifton and a lot of the guys knew them personally.

Anyway, Tommy's plan was to call Sandy over and tell her he had something in the box especially for her and when she looked in, he was going to push it in her face! Wow, poor Sandy, I thought!

Well, the corner of Beech Street and Delawanna Avenue in front of the Suburban Market was pretty crowded on that day as Sandy came walking up Beech Street towards the crowd of kids. Tommy ran to get his "gift" and was standing there as Sandy walked up. He said; "Hey Sandy, comear, (come here in NJ lingo) I got something for you." Sandy, being no fool, approached very warily while Tommy was telling her, "Hey, really, don't worry, it's a peace offering from me to you!"

Sandy very cautiously approached and then Tommy flipped open the lid, but just before he shoved it in her face, Sandy, now aware of what was going to happen, put her hands under the box and reversed Tommy's planned next step by pushing the box of blueberry preserves in his face! Sandy then turned and ran with Tommy in hot pursuit covered in blueberries and steaming mad because of the embarrassing outcome of his failed plan!

He never did catch her, as she was pretty quick on her feet. She was a pretty tough customer and the other girls all realized it when she beat-the-crap out of Dawn.

Dawn was a "Tom-Boy" and tough in her own way. She was also

very good-looking I might add, but she met her match the day she took on Sandy and got her "come-up-ins" in the same way Yonko did.

Sandy and Dawn weren't the only tough girls in Delawanna during that time and probably the toughest was a girl named "Burdie." I'm not sure what that was short for; Probably Bertha or something like that.

Burdie was in the older age group of kids, about three to four years older than us. She lived with Karen, a girl in our age group's family. Burdie always wore tight dungarees and a dungaree jacket and if you looked at her wrong, she wanted to fight you. She didn't care who you were, male or female!

The tight dungarees were lost on us at the time (sort of), but not the older guys (definitely not). We would hear them making comments about her in a way that was different from the way we felt about her. We were a little afraid of her, but they all said they wished she would try to tangle with them. We were somewhat perplexed by their perspective at the time, but, we eventually grew to have the same point of view on this topic and the things about their behavior, that we didn't really understand, started to make more sense to us. Before that change we were "looking out" for Burdie" and they were "looking for" Burdie! What a difference a few years makes in perspectives.

During those care-free days some of our free time would be spent over at the Delawanna Railroad station house located on Oak Street near the intersection of Delawanna Ave. The station master was a big, burly man named Van Sickle. He appeared to be in his late forties to early fifties.

Van always had a Lucky Strike cigarette dangling from his lips that moved up and down as he talked. It compelled you to watch the ash of his cigarette wondering when it was going to fall into his lap or all over the paper work that was scattered all over the top of his already untidy, roll-top desk. Ultimately that is exactly what happened causing him to have the same reaction each time, which consisted of many colorful expletives, mostly blaming God for the mess created on his desk.

This rail-road station was a passenger and package delivery pick-up stop for the trains running on the Delaware and Lackawanna Lines. (The combination of those two words (Delaware and Lackawanna) is how the name Delawanna was formed.)

Van would let us hang-out there…for a price. The price was; we had to help load and unload packages. Fair enough, we thought as we were always looking for something to do and somewhere to hang-out. He also included a stick of gum in the reward for our efforts; Big spender Van was!

Van was a master "ball-buster" to put it mildly and he was constantly making jokes and comments along with asking questions that often-times seemed to be over our heads intellectually or possibly un-intellectually. Whenever you gave a correct answer to one of his ball-busting questions, he would say, "Boy, you're a fart smeller…I mean a smart feller…ha,ha,ha!," or he would grab your leg and squeeze it with his huge vice-like hands and then laugh when you pleaded for him to let go!

He seemed to be fascinated by flatulence and was always "letting one rip" and then saying, "Whooaaa baby, what happened here?" He'd ask you to pull on his finger and then let one "rip," always laughing like it was the first time he did it! He would, at times, tell one of us to get something from his office after he just exited from there. When you walked in, you would almost lose your breath from a stench that was hard to believe came from a human being, then he would start laughing and say, "Gotcha, ah-ha-ha!"

He used to tell us that Rutt's Hut named the "Ripper" hot dog after him! That…we never believed, because if we did it would have ruined our desire to have the most famous hot dog in the world. But, I'll have to say, whenever I did have one, I thought of Van…that bastard, damned near ruin my taste for them!!!

Whenever the trains came in we would take one of the two package carts from the area behind Van's office, load them up and wheel them out to the tracks. Both carts had huge wooden spoke wheels with metal bands wrapped completely around the wheels circumference. One cart, the only one we used, had only two wheels and required you to balance it as you lifted up on the wooden handles to wheel it outside. The other cart had four wheels and the front wheels turned on a pivoting beam similar to a stagecoach and required it to be pulled by a vehicle or, most likely, a horse.

Both carts had to have been made in the late 1800s or early 1900s. Around the same time Van was born, we used to tell him, giving him reason to grab and squeeze your leg until you cried "Uncle" and promised you wouldn't do it again! He really wanted you to say it again so he would have a reason to chase you and inflict his revenge on you.

When the weather was bad, we would wait in the station house in the morning for the school bus that took us to Woodrow Wilson Junior High School at the other side of Clifton, you know…the side of Clifton that we didn't think or wouldn't admit really existed.

There were some mornings when someone would look out the station window and say, "Uh-oh, too late, the bus is leaving, oh well…no school today!" We would then walk home and hope nobody's mom offered to drive us to school, which wasn't likely to happen as most families only had one car. Van never said anything about us missing the bus, because he knew he would have free help for the rest of the day. But Van's free labor force was starting to thin out as the older guys now had their driver's licenses and didn't come to the station anymore. Also, the car-bug was starting to bite my friends and me…hard!

We were spending more and more time around places where there were cars being repaired and less time hanging out by Van. With almost no time spent with the Green Hornet Hot Rod Schwinn, which now lay all but forgotten in the corner of the shop behind my house. We rarely ever rode our bikes anymore because, in our minds at the time, bikes were for younger kids only! We didn't want the older guys to see us riding our bikes. We thought if they saw us on them, they would think we were just little pain-in-the-ass kids and not let us hang around observing their every action.

We split some of our time between Paul's Friendly Service and Delawanna Building Supply. With more and more of that time being spent at Paul's. We were, by now, convinced that George was not the guy for us to learn how to repair anything from. His lessons were always taken as how not to repair anything! We realized early on that, although we liked George a lot, he was pretty much a "butcher" when it came to repairing things. We would, however, stop by from time-to-time just for the humor of his outrageous ability to, as Joe, the owner of Delawanna Building Supply used to say, "That George can turn a perfectly cooked filet mignon dinner into a gigantic shit sandwich!"

Chapter Twelve:

Fill Up the Oil and Check the Gas Please and Odd Car Names

When Paul moved his gas station business from his original Richfield Gas station in Passaic NJ to the Main Ave. location in Delawanna he changed to Mobil Gas. We would hang-out there day and night, or as long as he would let us. We helped out as much as we could, but were probably in the way more often than not. Paul knew how preoccupied we were with anything that had to do with cars, so one day he said to Billy Walsh and I, "See those two old Fords back there?," referring to a Robins Egg Blue (non-original color) '51 Ford Deluxe Coupe and a Sheridan Blue '51 Ford Four-door sedan) well, if you guys want them, you can have them to fool around with." Want them?!...Holy crap!!...Of course we want them!

He said, the coupe had a bad engine, but the four-door should be ok, "After you get it running." Neither car had run for some time now. They were customer's cars that were turned over to Paul due to the cost involved in repairing them.

I always loved those '49 to '51 Fords. There were a lot of them around at the time and they were a favorite of teenage boys to modify or customize. My brother, John Jay, had a neat little '49 Ford convertible that was very typical of most of the kids cars in those days. It had skirts, was nosed and decked and had primer spots all over it. It was quite a thrill to go for a ride in that old Ford.

I guess Paul figured the cars would occupy some of our time and keep us out of his way for a while. What he didn't figure on though was how when he returned from a parts pick up that same day we had the engine half out of the four-door! He pulled up and said, "What the hell are you idiots doing?" We told him we were going to put the engine from the four-door into the coupe. I mean it only made sense to us; who the hell would chose the four-door over the coupe? Paul would, that's who!

He said, "Cheezuz Caahrist" (that's what it sounded like when he used that, his favorite cuss word). It would not be the last time I heard it from him either. As a matter-of-fact there were times I was beginning to think it was part of my name because it seemed that he used it as a prefix to my given name (Cheezuz Caahrist Bob!)

Anyway, he admonished us for "butchering" a perfectly good four-door to repair the coupe, which wasn't in as good condition. Our theory of "but it is a coupe" didn't fly at all with Paul. He just couldn't grasp our logic or lack of it as far is he was concerned. Paul just could not see the rationale in our decision to use the four-door car as a parts car. We tried to make him understand in the best verbal terms available to us teenagers at the time. To put things in our perspective to him we told Paul that the coupe, to us, was like going to the prom with one of the best looking girls in school and the four-door was like going to the prom with your sister! He just stood there for a moment staring at us and at first he said nothing. Then he turned and walked away with his, by now, all too familiar head shake and said, "You're both nuts"!

By the time we got up the nerve to walk inside Paul had his bottle of Segrams Seven out on the counter; The one he kept there for post encounters with the most aggravating of customers. He said, "You kids are going to drive me to drink!" "First of all, tell me how in God's name do you expect to pull those engines out in that back yard?" We said that we didn't think of that yet. He said, "Of course you didn't think of that!" "Cheezuz Caahrist!" Wow...we certainly pissed him off this time, I thought. But, we've done it before and we knew he would get over it soon...hopefully!

As we discussed the current situation with Paul old John from over on Clay Street pulled up to the pumps for gas in his 1953 Dodge Coronet Club Coupe. Paul looked up when he heard the bell ring said, "Ah Chezuz Caahrist, this is the last guy I want to deal with now!"

Now John was a nice old guy who was in his late seventies or early eighties, but he was one of those customers that always had a noise in his car that no one else could hear but him. And it always required Paul to take a ride with him and spend the next fifteen or twenty minutes trying to convince him everything was ok. Plus, Paul could never charge him, because he never really had to do anything to the car. He just wasted some of his time assuring old John that every thing was ok. Paul used to say, "He doesn't need a mechanic, he needs a new Goddamn hearing aid"!

Anyway, Billy and I offered to take care of John and his two-tone Riviera and Spring Green colored coupe to try to pull Paul back over to our side again on the Ford engine swap issue. Paul just said, "Yes, please do!"

When we approached his car, John told us to "Fill it up and add a quart of Quaker State HD 30-30w" then stated, "That's why I come here ya know"; "Because Quaker State is the best oil made ya know." He made that same statement every time he came in for gas...and oil!

(Paul sold Quaker State products because he owned the gas station and was an independent Mobil Oil dealer or he wouldn't have been allowed to sell anything but their products.)

As Billy went around to the back of the car to fill up the gas tank, I opened the hood, went to the oil rack grabbed a quart of Quaker State (the best oil made ya know), stuck the quart with the combination opener/spout and added the requested quart of oil to the flathead six cylinder motor. After the completion of these tasks I went in the office to ring up the total sale for the gas and oil of $3.10. Paul said to me, "Did I just see you add a quart of oil to John's car? I told him that I did add one at John's request. He then asked me, "Did you stick it?" (meaning to check the oil with the dip stick) to which I replied "No, I didn't." He said, "You'd better go out and stick it, because I added a quart two or three times lately at his request and the car doesn't seem to smoke at all!"

I went back out and John was still at the pumps telling Billy about a noise he thinks he heard on the way over for gas. I told John that I wanted to check the dip stick and when I did I found the oil mark almost at the top of the stick. I advised Paul of my finding and he promptly put the car up on the lift and drained out approximately four extra quarts of "the best oil made." Paul told old John that just because it was "the best oil made" didn't mean he had to add more than was required!

This incident got Paul out of the glum mood we had put him in with our "car butchering" episode for the time being, but he still wasn't on our side with "butchering" the four-door. As a matter-of-fact he told us to hold-off on doing any more to the Fords until he had time to digest the whole thing.

As we sat there in the office that day a dark gray-primered '50 Ford Deluxe two-door sedan with white-walls and full moon-discs that we had never seen before pulled in and parked over by the phone both at the far end of the lot. There were four kids in the car and from where we were we could see it had a name painted on the front fender, but we couldn't make out what it said.

Curiosity got the best of us, so Billy and I walked over to the car for a closer look. Two of the kids were out of the car and one of them was on the phone as we approached. When we got close enough we saw the name clearly, although it didn't make much sense to us at the time or ever for that matter. The name of the car was; "Logs Hollowin' Sound"! Yep, that's what was painted in red on the lower sections of both front fenders! I had no idea what that meant then, nor do I now.

I never saw any of the kids that came in with the car before. The owner, a tall, thin built, blonde haired guy with a crew-cut, started talking with Billy and I then opened the hood to show us the '53 Mercury flathead with Fenton aluminum heads and two, two barrel carburetors on an Eddie Meyer intake manifold. He told us the car was pretty fast and he raced it often. I asked him if he knew how to speed-shift and he said, "No, not really." I told him if he waited around for about an hour or so the "Speed-Shift King" of North Jersey would most likely be here and could possibly give him a lesson or two. He said that sounded like a good idea and he might just do that. I then asked him if he had any money with him. He said, "Why, does he charge for the lessons?" I told him that he did not charge for the lessons, but there was a chance that his car would not be drivable after the lesson and he may need to take a bus home. He replied, "Uh, on second thought, I think I'll pass on that lesson!"

He then told us that he had PA system in the car which he promptly showed to us. He removed the microphone from it's holder on the car's dashboard, put it to his mouth, and started making all kinds of inappropriate obscene comments that rang out loud and clear through the gas station lot and surrounding area.

After several of these comments Paul stuck his head out from the office and just stared at the kid. The kid got the hint and said," I guess I better get the f--k out here!

. He then jumped into "Logs Hollowin' Sound" said, "See ya" and disappeared down Main Ave. never to be seen again. That kind of thing seemed to happen often back then; you'd see a car once, then never see it again.

When we went back inside Paul asked, "Who the hell was that bucket of shit for brains?" We told him that we didn't know. It was the first time we had ever seen any of them before. Paul said, "Those guys make you guys look like scholars." Good timing, I thought. Looks like we could be inching our way back into favorable terms here.

Me on my uncle's Oliver Standard tractor that I drove once, and only once back in 1955.

Jimmy Rau (Pussy Foot) and his '55 Pontiac circa: 1959

Paul's '54 Chevy service truck.
Retired to the "bone yard" (1970s).
I made many parts runs in this truck.

My brother John Jay's '49 convertible.

1956 Oldsmobile grille

plus

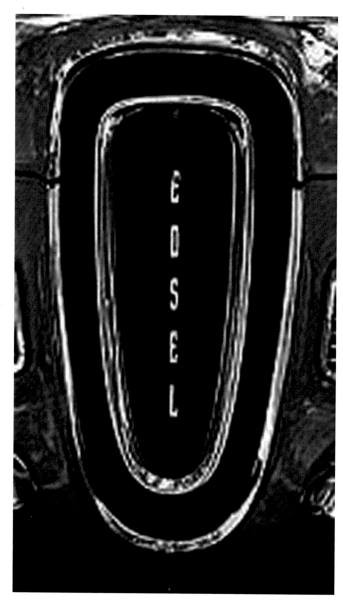

equals 1958 Edsel grille

1960 Edsel grille

1959 Pontiac grille

1959 Pontiac tail lights

1960 Edsel tail lights

1961 Plymouth tail light

1960 Edsel parking light
You be the judge!

The original "Buzzard II" 409/409. This car could run
along with the best of them.

Delawanna Reunion 2007.
L to R: Joe Mattiello, Me, Darlene,
Ronnie, Ted, Karlene, Phil, Sandy,
Paula, Tom Walsh, Tom Surowiec.

Chapter Thirteen:
Three Joe's and a Beast

As we sat in Paul's office, who pulls in next, but "Fat Joe" in his Terrace and Glen Green two-tone '52 Buick Special Riviera Coupe. The car actually would have been pretty nice looking if it was owned by someone else and not…Fat Joe! Fat Joe was a regular at Paul's; a regular pain-in-the-ass in our opinion! He would always drive to the rear of the lot and then go to sleep in his car; Usually with a mouth full of partially chewed peanuts and another bountiful portion in his hand just waiting to be shoveled in the oversized aperture of this enormous, inhuman eating machine.

Paul told us that Joe pretty much lived in his car and would go to the Y.M.C.A. whenever he felt the need to shower. Based on that statement, I can tell you that after being near him, he definitely was not on a first-name basis with anyone at the "Y"!

I never knew his last name; Not even sure if it wasn't Joe and perhaps his first name was actually Fat. If so, I commend his parents on being so perceptive as to his impending plumatatious future! But if it was only a nickname, I can tell you it was justly earned!

Paul said to us, "Now don't go and break his balls…please!" He made that request because when Joe would go to sleep we used to get behind the car and start rocking it up and down just to screw with him! When he would partially awaken, we would duck down behind the car out-of-sight. He would look around for a moment and go back to sleep.

On occasion Joe would have someone pick him up from Paul's and ask Paul to change the oil and lube the car while he was gone. (I used to say he better not stand too close to the garbage while he's waiting for a ride or he might end up in the big green truck with "Frank Stamato Refuse" written on the side.)

Whenever he did leave his car we would disappear because Paul would, at times, ask us to drive Joe's car into the bay and onto the lift. Although we would do almost anything to drive a car at that time, there were limitations to our enthusiasm, and driving Fat Joe's car reached that limit! I did it once, and that was enough for me! That car smelled like a hog farm on a hot August afternoon! It was disgusting to say the least and after I got out of the car I felt like Fat Joe's aura was now attached to me. That's all I needed at that time in my life. It was hard enough to have a girl interested in me and now I had Fat Joe's body secretions and odors all over me! *EEYUKK!!* No thanks…I'd rather go home and get the Green Hornet back on the road again! There were only so many girls in our age group in Delawanna and the girls from school were too afraid to come to Delawanna due to our much maligned reputation! Plus the girls from school all seemed to prefer the "jocks" and not the "gear-head" type that most of us were.

During the time that we hung out at Paul's we would earn money helping out here and there. Actually, we really would have helped out without any financial reward just for the privilege of being allowed to hang around a gas station. We would get tips here and there from cleaning windows at the pumps. Sometimes we got more than tips cleaning the windows when a woman would pull in for gas and was careless with attention to her modesty. There were certain female "regulars" that would cause a race between us to get to the fuel island for the opportunity to clean their windows!

Joanne, (everyone called her "Jo") a very-well-put-together female "regular" customer from Nutley, who was well into her forties, always had more "laundry" on display than a Sears and Roebucks catalog. She either got a kick out of watching us young guys trip over each other trying to get to her Apricot colored '57 Buick Special convertible for an "eye-full," or she was just completely unconscious as to the seductive powers she had on us. Possibly she just underestimated our peeking (no pun intended) sexual interest in women, no matter what age they might be!

Sometimes she would pull in and say, "Hi there boys, is Paul in?" "I need to speak to him about my car." Paul would always oblige her request and answer whatever it was she was concerned with that day. We noticed that when he finished talking to her and while walking away from her car, he gave that familiar head shake to the side. Did he think she was "nuts" too, like old John, or was he as impressed as we were with the exhibition before him? Were we now going to have to race Paul to the fuel island too? We never discussed this topic (sex) with Paul. How could we? We hung out with his daughter!

At any rate, there was a stark contrast between these two customers discussed here; Joanne and Fat Joe. One of them sent us running for the fuel island and the other one sent us running for the hills!

Another notable customer of Paul's was Pete Batist. Pete was in his early to mid-fifties at the time. He was a very nice guy that treated us kids, and everyone else with respect. He was one of the regulars over at Rivelli's Tavern on Oak Street. Pete was really a bit too regular though and that was his main problem. His nick-name was "Pete the Beast." I don't know how he got that name or who gave it to him, but I do know that whenever he pulled into Paul's with his Berkshire Green 1950 Pontiac Chieftain Four-Door Sedan everyone ran for cover, including Paul!

Pete had so many traffic mishaps with his car that there wasn't a straight panel to be found on the old Pontiac. Pete's car could be seen sitting in different locations for days at a time, because Pete often didn't know where he last left it. Half of the time he had to walk to work at the Waldrich Bleachery due to "misplacing" his car. He would tell us if we wanted to use the car to "just take it." We used to tell him we weren't old enough to drive and he would say, "Ah, don't worry about it!"

We never did take him up on his offer, as tempting as it might have seemed at the time. Good thing he never made that offer to Dean!

Pete was hard on himself due to his life-style, but he was gentle and kind to everyone else. Knowing him made me realize that in spite of his one self-destructive bad habit, he had enough good qualities in him to try to emulate.

To this day if you were to see an old picture of Delawanna, especially if there is a bar in the back-ground, you will most likely see Pete's old Pontiac sitting near-by like the trusty, old horse of a down-trodden, but reliable old cowboy.

Regardless of what we did or how much money we made while at Paul's we would always spend most of it at "Joe's Hot Dogs." Joe was a fixture on Main Ave. directly across from William Street and approximately three-hundred feet from Paul's Friendly Service. We just couldn't get through a day with out a couple of Sabrett hot dogs with mustard and some of Joe's home-made onions and sauce and an ice-cold Orange Crush soda.

Joe was in the same location for many years. Everyday he would drive his late 1930s G.M.C. delivery truck converted to a rolling kitchen from his house on Cherry Street over to "his" location. He never went over ten to fifteen miles-per-hour on this daily trip and he always had a string of cars behind him on his way down Delawanna Ave. blowing their horns, trying to get around him. But Joe never did anything but smile and wave at the unwilling, pissed-off entourage he unwittingly attracted, or maybe trapped, is a better word! Joe was part of the whole Delawanna experience for sure!

Chapter Fourteen:
Bo-Bo gives Jimbo a Boo-Boo and the Art of Un-stealing

When my friend Billy and I wound up with the '51 Chevy Fleetline Deluxe Four-Door Sedan that I wrote about in Hot rods, Pink-bellies and Hank Ballard, we relinquished our brief ownership of the '51 Fords. Both of these cars were later turned over to Paul's son, Tommy, who continued the butchery Billy and I started to perform on them until they were eventually sent to Pete Sadowitz's Auto Wreckers and Fine Used Cars.

You certainly would seem to be off to a bad start in the automobile department if you were you purchasing a car from an "Auto Wrecker"! The name implies that they are in the business of scrapping worn-out junk cars, not selling "fine" used cars! The word "fine" does not seem to fit anywhere within the boundaries of any of the wrecking yards I have seen.

Wrecking yards and wrecking yard owners in particular were/are a unique breed unto themselves, to say the least. They all must be related one way or another, because they all have the exact same personality traits and demeanor. They are either abrasive or extra abrasive! They always seemed to be pissed off! The usual greeting you could expect from any of the yard owners was, "What do you want?!" or "Get the Hell outta here kid, I got no time for this shit!" Excuse me sir it's "have no," not "got no" as in "I have no time for this shit!"! Yeah, I almost was going to say that…right!

There were, at the time, many auto wrecking yards in Clifton or within the immediate vicinity. There were two in Delawanna alone, unless you count the Blackson's back-yard on Delawanna Ave. In that case, there were three junk-yards in Delawanna! However, the only thing you could possibly get from the Blackson's "private junk-yard" was a good old fashioned ass-kickin' if you were caught back there by "Jimbo." I'm not sure if that was his real name, but that's what we called him. Jimbo was the nephew of the property owner! Now this guy could make a real junk-yard owner run for his life! I'm not sure how mean he really was, but he sure looked and sounded mean to us! However, that never stopped us from going down the hill behind his house to look over the many abandoned cars that were there. To be honest, it was sort of exciting to us when he came running down the hill to chase us. He never did actually catch any of us though; close, but he never was able to actually make physical contact, which was a good thing. We always had someone looking out for him as we climbed in and around cars like the faded "baby blue" colored 1939 Lincoln Zephyr Convertible Coupe that sat there in a deteriorated condition. That car was a favorite of ours to sit in and pretend we were driving.

Jimbo was a very large black man in his twenties or thirties. He was well over six feet tall and two-hundred plus pounds, very muscular with a deep gravely voice that made him sound mean as a Bull Dog! But, as we found out one day, he was also as dumb as a fence-post!

On that day he tried to sneak-up on Roy, Matt Dwyer and I as we were climbing through the cars. Normally he would come running from the house throwing the screen-door open while already screaming at the top of his lungs as he ran towards us. But after many unsuccessful attempts in our capture, he decided to use stealth and cunning instead of his usual loud and obvious approach. The problem with that tactic was that, although someone his size could easily be stealthy, someone with his intelligence could never be cunning.

Apparently when he saw us on this particular day he decided to go out the front door, go around to his next door neighbors house (the Wrights) and sneak-up on our flank. Pretty good plan, as we would never have looked for him there.

Well, as he came around the side of the Wright's house and slowly made his way to the rear yard using the garage to conceal himself from our field of view, he was being as stealthy and alert as he could possibly be. Then, as he rounded the back of the garage…he came upon an uncalculated obstacle; An even stealthier, much more intelligent and much more alert…Bo-Bo, the Wrights 80 lb *real* Bull Dog!!!

Bo-Bo was laying in wait for the approaching intruder and, being much brighter than Jimbo, was at the beginning of his leash-run with at least twenty feet of clear, unrestricted run ahead of him. When the time was right Bo-Bo did what he was paid to do; He charged the preoccupied, unsuspecting Jimbo with a Lion-like growl, which now attracted our attention to the scene that was about to unfold before our eyes. Jimbo's reaction was a little slow and as he turned to run old Bo-Bo sunk his canines into poor Jimbo's ass causing his former fearsome growling voice to now have an almost female falsetto pitch to it as he screamed from the fear and pain inflicted by the unrelenting Bo-Bo.

Jimbo finally broke free and ran into the house screaming. Then we heard his Uncle say to him, "Boy, you're a damned fool!" "What the hell is wrong with your dumb ass?" "You deserved to get your damn fat ass bit!" "I thought they were the fools for crawling through those damn cars, but you're the fool, not them!" Wow, first Jimbo got his ass chewed, then he got his ass chewed-out!

The cars that were available from places such as Sadowitz's yard were usually very reasonably price. For example Bruce Dixon bought a decent 1940 Buick Special Four-Door Sedan for a paltry $40.00 in 1960! The sedan still wore the original Silver French Gray enamel that it left the Buick factory with. The car ran and drove well and was quite a lot of fun to ride around in, even in those times. There were many cars that are very collectible today that were available for little and sometimes no money back then! No one realized it at the time though.

If you drove a twenty year old or older car back then, it had better have been a hot rod or custom; If not, it was just an old piece of crap to everyone else. Bruce's Buick fell into the latter category, but not to us younger guys. To us it was a pretty cool old car, but what did we know!

In those days it was a lot of fun snooping through the area junk-yards. Sometimes we would crawl through an opening in a fence in places like Delawanna Scrap Iron and Metal down off the River Road adjacent to the railroad tracks. You had to be careful though as some yard owners let dogs loose that were as mean as the owners themselves!

I remember seeing old Harley Davidson and Indian motorcycles from the 1930s and 40s just thrown on the junk pile or lying around the yard. We always wanted to take a motor from one of them to build a go-cart, but we never did. During one of our Sunday afternoon snooping excursions I found a pretty decent Schwinn bicycle at Delawanna Scrap and decided I would take it home. I guess we always thought that it was all junk, so it wasn't stealing if we took anything. Wrong! Within five minutes of getting home with the bike and showing it to my father, I was on my way back to Delawanna Scrap to "un-steal" the bike! Dad made me take it back and said, "Put it right back in the same spot that you took it from, it's not yours, never was yours and never will be yours unless you go down there tomorrow when they are open and buy it!" Another lesson learned; Taking someone's junk is still stealing!

Chapter Fifteen:
T.F.D.T.F. and Color Coordinated Girlfriends

In September of 1960 one of the older guys, Bruce Dixon, asked a few of us younger guys if we wanted to go to the drag races at Island Dragway, a newly opened track in Great Meadows, New Jersey. None of us had ever been to a drag strip before, so we jumped at the opportunity. We used to hear the older guys talk about a drag strip up in Montgomery, New York, but no one ever invited us to go along. Why would they? Even if they ever felt so benevolent, which they never did, we would be taking up a spot that a girl could fill.

Bruce said we had to start out early as it was a long drive…fifty miles! Wow, that sounded like a long way for kids like us who hardly ever ventured out of Delawanna!

We all met at Paul's gas station the following Sunday morning at 6:00am. There would be no church for any of us today. I thought about weather or not I would tell Father Dempsey at my next confession about missing mass to go to the drags, but quickly decided against it. Especially in light of the swearing rampage he went on during the pool table incident. He lost a little of his holy, priestly image somewhere between "You Goddamn little bastards" and "I'd like to beat your Goddamn asses!"

It was a little cool at 6:00am this late summer, early fall morning as Billy, Ted and I waited for Bruce to show-up. As we stood there talking we saw Bruce heading in our direction on Main Ave. in his Palasades Green '50 Ford Tudor Sedan. Bruce always seemed to have a different car. He went from older models to newer models and back to older models again. This Ford was his latest acquisition and eight years older than his previous car, the '58 Plymouth Plaza.

Billy and I were, at this time, the owners of one of his past road warriors, the '51 Chevy Fleetline Four-door sedan I mentioned previously in "Hot Rods, Pink-bellies and Hank Ballard. Bruce had quite a number of cars in a relatively short time span.

In between the '58 Plymouth, '40 Buick sedan, a '50 Olds 88 four-door sedan and the '50 Ford was a black '50 Mercury Monterey Coupe. One day while diving through Passaic's "downtown" shopping district with Bruce in the Merc we were hit broadside in the front passenger side door. Moments before impact, Billy, who was sitting in the front passenger seat, had just pulled his arm back into the car after having it dangling outside of the car for most of the trip. It was one of those times when we all laughed about what almost happened after the fact! Close call for Billy on that one!

Back to our trip to Island Dragway. We finally got under-way just as Kathy Young and the Innocents hit song "A Thousand Stars in the Sky" started playing on WMCA, and reached our destination of Hackettstown, N.J. one and one half hours later. We had to take Route 46 all the way from Clifton to Hackettstown, because at that time, Route 80 had yet to be completed. The dirt entry road leading from Route 46 in Hackettstown to the drag strip was backed up with cars and it took us about one half hour to get into the spectators side of the track.

As we were parking the car I saw two cars, a 1960 Chevy and a 1957 Chevy going down the track. That was the first sanctioned drag race I ever witnessed. The next car to run was a 1940 Willys coupe that I was familiar with that hailed from Nutley, N.J.(the next town to the south of Delawanna) it was owned by Novotny's garage and I had always heard it was a very strong runner. His opponent was a Pontiac powered street roadster called "The Whistling Tee-Pot" and owned by a fellow named Al Decker. It was a very close race with the Novotny's "Baby Cakes" pulling out the win at the top end.

At the time I wasn't all that familiar with what all the different engine options were that were available from the factories, but I did recognize a lot of the engines that I saw in the Street Roadster classes and other open engine cars from working at Paul's. The announcers would usually make mention of what engines the cars were running. That information was then stored in the "useless information folder" in the "selective memory file" of my brain…you know, the same brain that was unable to store information I was expected to recall…like important information given to me at…school! That is why I was given an additional opportunity to absorb the important information I seemed to have missed there; It was called "summer school"!

The one good thing about having this "selective memory affliction" is that many of my Delawanna friends had the same malady, requiring them to also attend summer school, which actually turned out to be a bad thing. The reason it was bad is because we talked about cars too often and once again struggled with pie are square (not unless it's a Sicilian Pizza we used to say!)

It's funny how in no time I memorized all the engine options for '59 and '60 Chevies and Fords and most of the other cars around at the time, but I had a hard time memorizing my school lessons. Back then the teachers would tell my parents; "Bob can do the work if he really wants to, but he's just lazy!" Lazy! I thought, yeah right, I just love going to summer school and then coming home to do my paper route and cut the grass! Plus working over at Paul's (get in Paul's way) and any other odd jobs I could find to make money.

I wasn't lazy I just had T.F.D.T.F. (too f'n distracted to focus) That's what they would call it today. Well maybe not exactly that, but they certainly would come up with a more politically correct acronym. Actually they did. It's now referred to as A.D.D. (attention deficit disorder) see how much better that sounds than "too f'n distracted to focus"!

Now that it actually is a clinically diagnosable affliction, I would have fallen into a totally different category. I would now have had the same teachers that hated me for being "lazy," feeling sorry for me due to my "affliction."

Anyhow, that day at the drags really did it for me in regards to my enthusiasm for anything automotive. The seed was planted a few years before by "The Ruby Rod," as I mentioned in Hot Rods, Pink-bellies and Hank Ballard, but now it was really taking hold.

The day after our trip to the drags while hanging out at Paul's a guy pulled in with a Snow-Crest White '59 Chevy Impala sport coupe. As the car pulled to the fuel island with the radio playing Maurice Williams and the Zodiacs iconic cruise song "Stay" at high volume, I notice that the front hood emblem had the "crossed flags" indicative of a "348" engine under the hood.

I quickly ran over to the car and looked inside at the Sapphire blue/green interior where I noticed the car had a floor mounted "spaghetti shifter" that I knew had to be a four-speed. Just before the driver shut the engine down I detected the sound of mechanical lifters telling me it was definitely one of the higher horse power versions of the 348 cubic inch engine. I also noticed the girlfriend of the kid that was driving; She was also one of the higher end versions of female companions I had seen recently!

Wow, was she ever good looking! She was a very petite brunette with her hair swept off to one side and held in place with a Robbins Egg blue colored ribbon that matched the super-tight short shorts that she was wearing! This along with the, very popular at the time, Capezio semi-flat heeled dancer shoe and a white Daisy Mae top with the top three buttons un-done! I thought, man, this guy has it all! His girlfriend even color coordinated her clothes to match his interior!

This was definitely one of God's cruel tricks that he played on teenage boys from time to time. Having a car like this pull in with a girl like that sitting inside! A moment like this is when your thoughts bounced back and forth hindering your ability to perform the simplest of tasks…like speaking! It was definitely a Jackie Gleason "homina, homina, homina" moment for sure! All this and then being expected to remember the "Gettysburg Address"…was too much for teenage boys to handle!

I'm not sure if I even heard the kid the first time he asked me to fill-er-up, but eventually I did and I tried to administer to the task at hand, but I kept feeling like I was walking around with my foot in a empty water bucket! It took every bit of my concentration just to be able to put one foot in front of the other!

Eventually the well-dressed kid wearing black "pegged" Chinos, a purple "three-quarter sleeve" shirt and Flag Brothers "Snap Jack" shoes got out of the car. I thought to myself at that time that the only thing I had in common with this guy is that I once had a pair of Snap Jack shoes. But I didn't even have them anymore! The thin little rods that ran up the length of the "hinged" tongue that comprised part of the closing mechanism jammed and were subsequently damaged to the point that they would no longer close, thereby bringing my father's prediction that "There is no way these pieces of crap are going to hold-up" to fruition!

Anyway, the kid walked around to the front and opened the hood. That's when I noticed the three chrome "pots" (air cleaners). I now knew it was Chevrolet's Super Turbo-Thrust 315 horse power version of the 348 due to the "three-twos" and the solid lifter camshaft. (I still, however, didn't know a damn thing about square pies that weren't pizzas or President Lincoln's Gettysburg Address, which as far as my friends and I were concerned, it could have been his summer get away home!)

The kid/owner of this car had a friendly demeanor and was open to talking about his car, which he had only recently purchased. I actually knew more about the engine specifications of his car than he did. He said that he thought about taking it to the track to "see what it could do."

I told him of our recent trip to Island Dragway and that I saw cars similar to his running in the low to mid fourteen second range at about ninety-five to one-hundred miles per hour. As I discussed the engine with him I couldn't help but notice his girlfriend as she leaned forward in the seat and kept pushing the radio buttons changing the channels back and forth from WMCA to WINS to WABC, not that it really mattered, as they all played the top forty songs all day long anyway. She finally stopped changing stations when she found "Blue Angel" by Roy Orbison playing then sat back in the seat appearing contented with that selection. I loved Roy Orbison's music and normally would really have enjoyed this song, but I enjoyed watching her lean forward to change the stations more.

I then noticed that Roy decided to come out and "help" by cleaning the windows. The kid told Roy that he didn't have to do that as he just washed the car, but Roy, as he sheepishly glanced over at me replied, "Ah don't worry it's no big deal." I knew, and I'm sure the kid knew why Roy was so benevolent!

After the car was filled the kid jumped back inside and started the engine and said, "Take it slow" as he pulled away from the pumps and out onto Main Ave. heading towards Route 3 in his high-performance Chevy. When he got half-way through first gear he punched the throttle to the floor causing all three Rochester 2G carburetors to eventually open with assistance from the vacuum reservoir mounted under the rear section of the left front fender. This created an exciting sound effect as the air rushed into the three fully opened ventures along with the squealing of the 7.50x14 tires that were now melting their way down Main Ave.!

It was all a very cool experience and I was totally envious of this guy for sure, oh well, maybe some day! But right now it was time to tend to Big John, the truck driver from Nutley who just pulled up to the pumps with his green, gas powered 1959 White Mustang tractor and flat-bed steel hauler trailer in tow. Probably on a return trip from the Bethlehem Steel Company in Allentown, Pennsylvania. As ambitious as Roy was previously, I noticed he didn't rush out to clean John's windows!

Chapter Sixteen:

*Can I Get that Bumperette in Size 40 Triple D Please
and Possibly a Song with a Good Beat?*

The urge to drive, for us guys, was really taking a strong hold now and was definitely interfering with the ability to concentrate on school work. That must be another reason why the girls always seemed to do better than us guys as we got older. It wasn't just the DDT form the mosquito sprayer. The guys had a lot more distractions than the girls did. I mean the girls liked the cars alright, but they weren't consumed with them in the same way we were. They knew nothing about engines and transmissions, nor did they care to know. They only knew colors. They were/are definitely a different breed and that's why they have separate entrances to schools.

They did, however, know which cars were cool and which cars weren't, there-by putting even more pressure on us guys to make sure that, not only did we pick a car that would satisfy our personal needs, but also one that they thought was cool! Way too much pressure for the guys! After all, we were also trying to impress them with everything from what we did, how we dressed, what we said, etc. etc. In their own way the girls did the same, I guess, but not in the same obsessive way, and not with the car thing going on at the same time!

I'm not even sure what comes first; Is it the cars for the love of cars or is it cars for the love of girls?! One of my friends, Bob Ferenzi, once told me that everything a guy does in his life from what he wears to what he drives etc., is for one thing only and one thing only…to attract girls! Who knows, maybe he's right! If that's the case, it sure is a hell of a lot cheaper to be a girl! I mean what do they have to spend money on…make-up, clothes and some accessories. They don't have to worry about the huge expense of, not just a car, but a cool car. You know, a car that supposedly is an extension of yourself. If and when the girls bought a car, it could be any car at all; Two-door, four-door, six-cylinder, automatic, whatever. It really didn't matter to the guys what kind of car they owned. Guys never judged girls on the cars they drove, but we were somehow subconsciously convinced that we were being judged by them, and everyone else by what we drove.

That being said, I think back in horror at the image I must have portrayed with my first legal street-driven car; A 1954 Oldsmobile Ninety-Eight four-door sedan!!! There is no question that my selection of wheels came down to economics. No ifs-and-or-buts about that! At least I hope that was the only reason I bought that car! I certainly hope it wasn't that I subliminally chose that beast of a car because I thought that it best represented the image I wanted to portray! If so, I was starting at the wrong end of the life-cycle by wanting to be some girl's grandfather rather than a boyfriend!

There were guys that didn't seem to have this problem of constantly being focused on cars and girls, but I wasn't friends with any of them. I know they existed; Not many of them, but they were around. I saw them at school everyday. I just don't know how they did it. They were able to focus and do well in school with relative ease and they could care less about cars, or girls for that matter, or at least that's the way it appeared to my friends and me. Who knows, maybe it has to do with what side of the brain you are using.

The guys that didn't care for cars sometimes wound up consciously choosing to drive cars similar to what the girls drove. It was just transportation to them; That was it, there was no more to it for those guys!

I don't know how they escaped the lure of cars back in that time period though. How could you not get caught up in the automotive frenzy? Every direction you turned cars and the importance of having a cool or fast one was being portrayed from the music we listened to, to the movies and television shows we watched.

There were early Rock and Roll songs from the 1950s about cars like; Chuck Berry's—Maybellene; Commander Cody and the Lost Planet Airmen's—Hot Rod Lincoln; Jackie Brenston and His Delta Cats—Rocket 88 and then the early '60s songs by groups like the Beachboys—Little Deuce Coupe, Don't worry Baby, 409, Spirit of America etc., etc.

Television shows like; 77 Sunset Strip with Edd (Kookie)Byrnes' character, "Gerald Lloyd Kookson the Third" driving around in the unbelievably cool Norm Grabowski owned '56 Dodge Royal Blue, '52 Cadillac powered T-Bucket.

Also, Route 66 with George Maharis and Martin Milner traveling around the country in a Corvette in their respective roles as Buz Murdock and Tod Stiles helped fuel the passion for cars in both young and old.

The older guys were all caught up in it. My friends and I were also caught up in it. It was a crazy, fun time to say the least. Starting in the mid fifties the automobile manufacturers gradually raised the horse power ante each year. Their high-performance advertising was aimed at teenage boys and young adult males exclusively. The ads didn't show young girls picking up their boyfriends in their new 1960 Chevrolet 335 horse power, 348 cubic inch Impala with four-speed transmission and three two barrel carburetors! No, they always showed a teenage or young adult male at the wheel of one of these high-performance cars, because of the testosterone-fueled mind-set of that particular age group.

Now this type of advertising on the automobile manufacturers part appears to lend credence to my friend Bob's analysis that everything you do in life is to attract girls! Seems the car makers did some analyzing of their own and agreed with Bob's thoughts on the subject!

All of this added even more pressure, in financial terms, to my friends and me. Here the automobile manufacturers were showing you what you needed to buy in the way of a car in order to be popular; Especially with the girls, and that's where all the pressure came in.

When I started to drive in 1962 I really wanted / needed a brand new 406 powered Galaxie or a 409 powered Impala or Belair, but all I could scrap up was $65.00 for a 1954 Oldsmobile ninety eight four-door! Pretty piss poor start in the "trying to attract girls department" I'd say!

Sex even came into consideration in automobile styling and design in, mostly in subliminal terms, but not always. Sometime it was right in your face like the G.M. stylist, Harley Earl's "Dagmar" bumper design (named after the statuesque, blonde TV star of the same name) starting on early'50s Cadillacs.

The large "bullet shaped" bulges that adorned the front end treatment of these cars was said to be aimed at male buyers with the subliminal image of female breasts being depicted (hence, the

Dagmar tag). That is very possibly a true story. I mean, it's a safe bet that more of these popular cars were sold by the bumpers conjuring up images of Dagmar than they would have if they resembled…let's say, Jimmy Durante's nose! I'm definitely betting my money on the mammaries winning out over the shnozola!

Assuming the premise of subliminal messages in advertising and design was accurate, then what was Ford thinking about when they designed the '57, '58 & '59 Edsels? Was that grille design supposed to take you back (mentally) to the womb or something? Maybe if you were a calf it might have, but it didn't worked on the male human as evidenced by their terrible sales numbers!

Whatever that grille design was supposed to do, it didn't! We used to say the grille looked like a '56 Oldsmobile sucking a lemon. If that was done intentionally by the Ford designers, then they definitely got the "sucking" part right!

And what about the 1960 Edsel? What the hell was that all about? The designers of the 1960 Edsel must have been in such fear of losing their jobs that they completely forgot all the rules of design! They took the 1960 Ford, which I happened to like although it didn't meet with rave reviews from most of my peers, and then they just threw parts at it in a last ditch effort to sell it as a newly designed Edsel just to keep the name alive when, in reality, they should have stuck a lemon in the grille and buried it!

It appeared as though Ford bought up all of Pontiacs left-over '59 body parts, reworked them slightly, and then bolted them onto a 1960 Ford! As proof of this, I offer the grille and taillights (turned on end). There is also the distinct possibility that they bought pre-production '61 Plymouth taillights from Chrysler and bolted them onto the front fenders; Possibly while they were being loaded up on the delivery trucks on the way to the dealers! Either that, or they sold them to Chrysler for the '61 Plymouths after Edsel went belly-up!

The drooping stainless side trim strip? Who knows? I am at a loss as to the origin of those! Possibly from a Chris Craft boat? Where ever they got them, I know they bought a lot of them, because they made it onto every model in the line-up…unfortunately! The term "line-up" was fitting for the 1960 Edsel as it brings to mind an execution by a firing squad!

The 1960 Ford, at least, had a very tranquil, smooth flowing design. By comparison, 1960 Edsel had all the flowing tranquility of a Picasso painting at a schizophrenia convention! It was horrible to say the least! It certainly did not conjure up any images of sex. Unless of course you considered the fact that if you bought one, you were pretty much *f--ked* if you thought you were going to be looked at as cool! All of this Edsel criticism and speculations are, of course, only my opinion.

I would rethink my criticism of the 1960 Edsel somewhat after I bought the '54 Oldsmobile ninety-eight. I mean, I have to admit that even an Edsel was perhaps slightly cooler than that four-door Olds. Not a four-door Edsel mind you, but a two-door hardtop or convertible might have been slightly cooler. I say might, because at least with the Olds most people probably thought that I couldn't afford anything any better, which was the absolute truth. But if you had a fairly new 1960 Edsel they probably would have assumed that you bought it out of choice, and that would certainly not be an image you'd want for yourself.

See how important it was to have the right car. You had to think out all of the options. Very few guys could get by with a dorky car that they bought by choice and not be ridiculed by their peers, plus not have it get in the way of impressing the girls. There was only one guy I knew of that got away with it, and that was Phil, fondly referred to by us as "Phil the Whore," for his mistaken use of the latter part of his permanent nick-name .

Now Phil liked cars alright, but he wasn't "nuts" over them like most of the rest of the guys in Delawanna and, I assume, the rest of the country were at the time. He did like Italian sports cars, but I think that came from his being born in Italy and his familiarity of those cars. He didn't like them enough to own one though.

Phil's first car was a Corvair! And it wasn't even a "Spyder"! See what I mean. None of the other guys in our group could have gotten away with buying a Corvair, but Phil could and did!

Phil was a laid-back guy that never really got into many controversies or arguments. He got along with everyone; Even guys from the other parts of Clifton. He wasn't outspoken or aggressive and he didn't have an ego problem at all. He never really talked about cars all that much, but he always went along with what everyone else wanted to do weather it involved cars or not. Those traits enabled him to always be looked at as a pretty cool guy…in spite of his Corvair purchase.

Phil was one of the few guys that just always seemed to fit in no matter what. Other guys would have been ridiculed for buying a Corvair or similar car. I guess based on individual expectations, Phil got a pass on any "Corvair heckling" because of the unique classification he fit into as a person. He definitely did not suffer from any low self esteem issues, quite the contrary in fact. All-in-all, he probably saved a lot more money than the rest of us.

I submit these photos as evidence that, in my opinion, the 1960 Edsel was most likely built from left-over Pontiac and Plymouth parts!

As I stated before, the music also played a huge part in what we did, or at least wanted to do, and the car builders knew that all too well. Even today certain songs make a now senior citizen hot rodder like myself feel like burning the tires down the street and banging the gears! Why is that…I don't know. But I do know that, as I stated previously, music is a very powerful stimulant, both in how it affects your mood at the particular time the "right song" is played, and also in how it brings back into recall small slices of time from your past in great detail. It does that for me and a lot of other people I talk to on that subject. I sometimes can't recall what I did yesterday without some pondering, but I can tell you exactly where I was, what I was doing and who I was with me the first time I heard "There's a Moon Out Tonight" by Nick Santo and the Capris, and that would only be one of many, many other examples, probably hundreds!

There are songs that remind me of each and everyone of my friends. Sometimes multiple songs can remind me of one person and a particular place in time. It's crazy how the human mind works. I wish I could have used the song recall to assist me with my school studies, but the A.D.D. (he's just lazy) thing would surely have kicked in. Frankly, I think it only works with people places or things you remember fondly. You know…the good nouns!

Thankfully, I can't think of any songs that remind me of someone I don't like. Wait, there is one, Joey Dee's "What Kind of Love is This" reminds me of the time two of us, (Pete Pach and I) were "jumped" at the St. Clares C.Y.O. dance by about eight "hop heads" from the other side of Clifton.

These guys were the first drug users I knew of. They definitely were not car guys. They couldn't be, because they spent all of their money (whenever they might have actually worked) on drugs, pretty clothes and long, black "trench coats." They really were the anti-hot rod / car type. Their whole lives (albeit a drastically short version) revolved around drugs.

Anyway, for no reason other than they were shit-bird drug addicts, they surrounded Pete and me at the dance and then jumped us. We had no time at all to react. They also actually punched and kicked the priest, Father Core, who tried to intervene into the foray. Just shows how drugs can turn people into a real scum-bags! They struck fast and then ran away like the titwillow, cowards they really were.

Pete and I then headed to Dunney Park for reinforcements, because as I stated, at that point it was just him and me and about eight of them. We scoured the neighborhood and came up with two of the shit-birds trying to get out of town. As it turned out the rest of their dirt-bag friends scattered in all different directions and left without them. We didn't do anything physically to the two, now whimpering little shit-heads. We couldn't have, or we would have been just like them, because we now out-numbered them at the same ratio they outnumbered us one half hour before. They were pretty-much just ridiculed for being "chicken-shit hop-heads" and sent on their way. They never returned to Delawanna after that and we always made sure that when we went to the C.Y.O. dance, we went with more the just two guys.

In proving that it is much better to spend your time and money on cars than on drugs; these guys, almost all of them, if not all of them, are dead, and have been for twenty to thirty years or longer!

Even though Joey Dee's song reminds me of that negative incident, I still do like it. Go figure! It is, however, the only song I can think of that brings to mind a negative incident.

Ok, I know, you're waiting for me to tell you where I was and who I was with when I first heard "There's a Moon Out Tonight" aren't you? Well, I was at Dunney Park in Delawanna when my friend Paula Surowiec, (Friendly Paul's daughter and one of the girls in the group I hung out with), was excitedly telling a group of us of a great new song that just came out called; "There's a Moon Out Tonight by The Capris." None of us had heard the song before, then within the very next few minutes it started playing on Paula's red and white Silvertone model 8212 portable radio that she never left home without.

Paula started yelling, "This is it, this is the song I was telling you about," we all listened intently, and at it's conclusion, had to agree that, in fact, it was a great song. I was there that day with about seven to eight other kids and every time I hear that song I think of Paula, her portable radio and the bleachers at Dunney Park.

Chapter Seventeen:
Beer Here!

Anyway, I got a little ahead of myself in the time chronology of all of this and I now have to back-up a little. As I stated, the car frenzy was in full swing and none of the guys in the group I hung out with were driving as of yet. The desire to drive didn't just hit us hard; It hit a lot of the kids in school at the same time.

Some of the guys from the Allwood section were a little more impatient than we were and used to go over to the Fette Ford's used car lot on Bloomfield Ave. and take the used cars for a "joy-ride"! The words "take the car for a joy-ride" seems to have a mitigating overtone to it. What they actually did was "steal" the cars, drive them around all night, and then put them back!

It was easy to do, especially if it was a Ford. All you had to do was run a jumper wire from the battery positive to the ballast resistor before the ignition coil and then use a screw driver to short the starter solenoid and the car was running! G.M. cars were also simple to "jump" back then and just required a slight bit more effort.

These guys even had cars that they claimed were "theirs." They tried to take the same car each night and they would get very upset if the car was "sold out from under them"! My friends and I were all to "chicken" to even think of trying something like that. Sipping Canada Dry sodas from the soda machine at De Camp Bus Lines was stressful enough and it was about our limit into the world of pilfering. Not that we didn't practice other mischievous deeds from time to time, but stealing a car was definitely out!

One summer day, I guess spawned out of boredom while waiting for the time to pass to obtaining a driver's license and independency, we decided to have a beer party over at Tom's house. Having the party in itself wasn't a problem, but specifying the party as a "beer party" presented it's own unique problems in that first, we needed beer! Second; you couldn't buy beer in the New Jersey unless you were twenty-one years of age! Third; none of us were even close to being twenty-one years old!

So, we thought long and hard and came up with a plan to order the beer from a liquor store and have it delivered. We then called Franzoni's Liquor Store in Passaic Park and ordered a case of Riengold Beer. About thirty minutes later the delivery man showed up at Tom's door, which by the way was directly across the street from Clifton Fire Engine #4's fire house on Delawanna Avenue.

Anyway, the delivery man rang the bell and Ronnie answered the door. Now the guy saw right away that Ronnie was not old enough to purchase beer and said to Ronnie, "Did someone order beer from this address?" To that Ronnie said' "Gee, I don't know, it must have been my father. He's upstairs in the shower right now." Ronnie then yelled up the stairs, "Hey Dad, did you order beer from Franzoni's?" (Now here is where it either all comes together or the guy leaves and takes the beer order back to the store). Tom, in the most grown-up voice he could muster up, yelled back down the stairs from behind the closed bathroom door, "Yes I did son, but I'm in the shower. I left the money on the coffee table." Ronnie turned to the table, picked up the money and handed it to the delivery man, who had a very strange look on his face like he wasn't all that sure about any of this.

In an obvious sort of reluctancy, the guy set the beer down, took the money from Ronnie and walked back to his black '58 Chevy sedan delivery. He sat in the vehicle for a few moments staring back at the house, looking through the screen door. After seeing that Ronnie had just walked away from the case of beer, he was a little more confident in the validity of the transaction and he just drove off.

The plan worked! How great is this, we thought, as we all came in from hiding on the back porch and made our way to the front door?! Not too great at all as we noticed some of the firemen standing out in front of the firehouse watching the whole thing! As we grabbed the beer, we could see them pointing to Tom's house and talking. "Damn! Do you think they know what we did?" Ronnie asked. "To late now," someone replied.

We convinced ourselves that maybe they really didn't see what happened and if they did, maybe they wouldn't say anything to Tom's dad.

Wrong...on both parts! They did see it and they did tell Tom's father. Fortunately for us Toms Dad, Lenny, was a pretty cool, laid-back kind of guy that liked all of us kids. He never spoke to us in an authoritative manner and would just voice his displeasure in a way that made us feel like we let him down if we did something wrong. That was what he did in this case also. He said he wouldn't tell the other parents this time, but if we did something like that again he would have to. That was fair enough for us and we never tried that trick again.

After all was said and done, we only had about one and one half beers apiece, due to the amount of kids that showed up.

I can still remember the Rheingold beer jingle though, word for word, all these years later! (*My beer is Rheingold the dry beer—think of Rheingold whenever you buy beer* and so forth and so on). Subliminal advertising at work again! It worked on us back then. Why else would we have picked that particular brand?! We definitely graduated from Cheerios! Not that it was a good thing!

That was the first and last of the beer parties for quite a while after our promise to Tom's father. Actually that wasn't the first beer party now that I think of it. It was the first one for me though. There was one party before that also took place at Tom's house, but I couldn't attend, because I had to help my mother paint the house! Maybe it was just as well that I had to, but I can remember the anxious feeling I had while helping her paint and knowing the party was going on...whew, that was tough! But what was I going to tell her, I couldn't help, because I wanted to attend an underage drinking party? Plus, it would have left her to paint the whole damn house by herself. As it was she would climb the ladder to do the top sides of the two-story, fairly large duplex home, because I had a fear of height.

At that party the ingenious idea of ordering the beer to be delivered hadn't been thought of yet. The supply of beer came from all of the attendees bringing a can or two of beer from their father's or mother's supply (it seemed a lot of the mothers back then liked to throw back a couple of Shlitz (when you're out of Shlitz, you're out of beer) or Schaefers (the one beer to have, when you're having more than one).

Nothing of any consequence came of that party though, so I didn't miss much, but at the time, you couldn't have convinced me of that while as I reluctantly dipped the large camel hair brush into the messy oil-base maroon paint, *yuk!*

At that first party, my friends weren't seen by the firemen across the street. They (the firemen) certainly did have lots of free time in those days except for the occasional torching of "Chalk Hills." Chalk Hills was a large empty parcel of land that had mounds of plaster covered dirt formed as a result of an explosion of the Kelly Plaster Board Company sometime in the 1930s.

These fields had lots of tall four foot high "Elephant Grass" (not sure if that is what it really was, but that's what we called it) growing on a large portion of it. Whenever that grass became dry, someone inevitably decided it was time to see the firemen of Engine #4 pull out in their 1947 Ward La France fire engine and do what they got paid to do.

They always quizzed us as to who the culprit was, as quite often we hung out in the firehouse. (They would let us hang out there and in turn we would buy soda and candy from their part-time "confectionary business") Most of the time we would hear who set the fields on fire, but we wouldn't say who it was, because, unlike the firemen themselves in the beer party incident, we didn't want to be labeled as squealers!

Chapter Eighteen:
I Think I'll Go Out For a little Push and to Oil or Not to Oil? That is the Question.

As I stated the desire to own, drive, race, or just look at and learn about cars was at a boiling point with my friends and me. My friend, Rich Prince, who lived in Passaic at the time, owned a 1929 Chevrolet sedan with several of his friends. Now this car didn't run, so they got it for twenty-five dollars! They used to spend their time taking turns pushing each other around an eight block area of Passaic! They pushed this thing up a grade for three blocks, over one block, let it roll down three blocks, over one block and then started all over again!

They thought that because it wasn't running, it would be legal to just push it around! Wrong! After getting stopped, initially for obstructing traffic, they were told it was still a motor vehicle and it had to be registered, insured and operated by a licensed driver only! They were let off the hook as far as any legal action was concerned, but were forced to sell their 3000lb soap box derby car at a five dollar loss!

Tom Walsh decided to try something similar, but not with a car that needed to be pushed. His car of choice was the often stolen '54 Chevrolet Belair four-door sedan owned by Ted's Mom. Tom knew that Ted used to, at times, set the ignition switch to off so it could be turned to on without the key, enabling the car for a quick "joy ride" around the block. Ted was no longer taking joy-rides in this car himself having been recently caught and punished for doing so, but he would set the ignition switch "just in case."

After starting the car and talking Ronnie into going along for a short ride, Tom headed down Linden Ave., made a left on William Street, drove to the intersection of Oak Street, made a left for the short block and then a left on Delawanna Avenue. So far, so good. Tom was just starting to feel comfortable and gaining in confidence, but then he looked in the rear view mirror and both of those feelings were quickly replaced by that icy-cold and tingling feeling of fear when he saw the black and white 1960 Pontiac sedan owned and operated by the Clifton Police Department directly behind him with the red "bubble-gum" roof mounted light turned on.

Tom now realized this illuminated light was meant for him and wisely pulled over directly across the street from the Suburban Market. The officer asked Tom for his license and registration and after some initial diversionary conversation, Tom admitted that he didn't have a license and was, in fact, underage.

Unfortunately for Tom neither of the officers in Clifton Police post car #7 (which was the "post car" for Delawanna) was Officer Joseph Padula. We had all gotten to know Joe pretty well, and he had a very good way with us kids. We all had a lot of respect for him in return. If it was Joe, he might have called Tom's Dad to pick him up and just given Tom a good talking to, (maybe) but it wasn't him, so the chips would now fall where they were going to fall.

As Ronnie sat in the rear of the police car he observed his mother coming out of Howard's Liquor Store next door to the Suburban

Market, so he slid down in the seat so she wouldn't see him. Nothing really happened to Ronnie as a result of this escapade. But Tom's punishment was a delay of six months in obtaining his driver's license when he turned seventeen.

All-in-all it wasn't worth it for a short joy ride, but it was irresistible to Tom at the time. Ted's Mom made sure that the car was always put on "lock" from that point on and warned Ted that he had better not pull any more stunts with her car's ignition switch or she would make sure that he didn't get his license either!

Moving ahead to February of 1961when George Harding got his driver's license. His first car was a black and white '57 Ford Fairlane 500 two-door hardtop. It was a pretty sharp looking car. It wasn't fast by any means as the Fordomatic transmission was not built with performance in mind (actually, I don't think it was built with anything in mind other than to take up the space between the engine and the differential).

The Ford was pretty dependable other than the, common to Ford "Y" blocks, valve-train oiling problem. At first George would stop the car periodically, remove the valve covers and physically oil the rocker arms! This became an obsessive ritual at least a couple of times a night and George ran around with the valve cover nuts hand tight for easy removal. He certainly didn't have to worry about them leaking as there was never any oil there anyway.

Several attempts were made by George to improve the oil or lack of oil condition, but to no avail. At the time George worked at the Waldrich Bleachery in Delawanna and while there he befriended an older guy, Ed Ayers, who claimed to have some mechanical aptitude. He convinced George of the proper way to address the rocker arm oiling situation and had him bring the car to his house to perform the repairs needed…in Ed's opinion that is!

We used to go there and watch Ed work on George's car and

then bust George on our observations of Ed's mechanical ability. We would say, "You know George, Ed isn't a very fast. He also isn't very slow. He seems to fall somewhere in the middle, I would say he's just half-fast! "Ha, ha, very funny," George would reply.

I will say one thing, George definitely had the cleanest valve covers around after the many times they were removed and cleaned!

After numerous attempts by Ed to regain oil flow it was determined that an "outside oiler kit" was needed. We all said that from the start, but Ed tried to tell George it could be repaired the right way. I'm not sure what that way was as we had all pretty much thought it was some design flaw in the engine and it was a waste of time to do anything, but install the oilers. So, the oiling kit was purchased from Pep Boys in Passaic and installed on the, otherwise decent running 212 horse-power 292 cubic inch "Y" block.

As I said before George's '57 wasn't very fast. That's why I was very surprised one day as we were traveling on Route 3 east-bound in the '57 and who pulled up next to us for a "kick-down" race? None other than…Jack Jorg (the Speed-shift King) in his Buick powered '51 Chevy, "The Chevick."

Jack was alone in his car and George had Ronnie, Tom and me as passengers. Jack motioned for George to go; With that, George dropped the Fordomatic in to low (which was just about right at the 50mph speed we were traveling at, because Lord knows they were geared too high for any kind of low-speed performance).

Anyway, George then "punched it" and jumped out a half fender length on the blue and white '51 Belair. They ran up to 90mph and all the Buick motor could do was pull the little Chevy coupe up about a half car length ahead of George. We realized that if George had been by himself and without the added weight of three passengers, he would probably have beaten the legendary Chevick!

Not a good showing for the Buick powered Chevrolet for sure.

The good news was that all transmissions in attendance managed to survive Jack's appearance. The only thing Jack blew on that day was the old Chevick's reputation!

One night during the next week or so, we pulled into the Tydol, Flying "A" station on the corner of Broadway and Vanhouten Ave. in Passaic for gas. While we were there fueling up a guy pulled in with a "Titian Red" '40 Ford Deluxe coupe. The guy driving was around nineteen or twenty years old and yelled across the fuel island at us, "Hey, you wanna race that Ford?" George said, "Is your forty stock?" The guy brings a pint bottle of Smirnoff Vodka to his lips, takes a big "swig" and says, "Yeah, right, why would I ask you to race if it was stock?"

I thought, this guy looks and sounds like a loose cannon. Drinking vodka while he's driving, he must be nuts! I then asked him what his car had under the hood. He took another swig out of his Smirnoff bottle then got out of the car and opened the hood. Wow, a Chrysler hemi rested in the area once occupied by the original 221 cubic inch, 85 horsepower flathead V/8 engine! I asked him which Chrysler engine it was, as there were several different cubic inch displacements since the "hemis" inception. He replied, "How the f--k would I know, I didn't put it in. I bought it this way." Man, I thought, this guy is a "winner" for sure. I then asked what transmission it had, but he didn't know the answer to that either! The engine had a single four-barrel carburetor and he said he thought it came out of a '56 Chrysler, so I figured it was the 354 cubic inch 280 horsepower version based on the knowledge I had acquired up to that point in time, which was a lot more than he seemed to have acquired. I guess it's pretty hard to accumulate much knowledge about anything when you ride around by yourself slugging down vodka straight from the bottle!

The Forty Ford also still had the shifter on the steering column, so I thought it probably still had the stock Ford driveline. I confirmed that when I looked under the car and saw the torque tube connected to the stock forty Ford rear end.

The first thing I noticed about the engine installation was that it didn't have a cooling fan. The nub of the water pump shaft sat in a little divot that appeared to have been hammered into the radiator cooling fins for clearance! I thought, man, I don't think Ted and I would have even done something like that! I asked him if it overheated and he said, "Yes." Well, at least he knew the answer to that question!

He asked again if George wanted to race and then specified, No money, just for shits and grins." George accepted the challenge to race for free, but said he wanted to do it at "kick-down" speed, to which the guy agreed.

As we pulled out of the station, I saw the guy hit the Smirnoff again and then do a pretty good "burn-out" as he headed down Broadway in the direction of Route 3. He "wound-up" first gear and then just let off causing the car to slow rapidly under the Hemi's compression with the dual "Smittys" rapping off. I guess it's hard to shift when you have a bottle of Smirnoffs in your hand and the other hand is on the steering wheel!

George, with Tom, Ronnie and me in tow, got on the highway (Rt. 3) heading east and waited in the slow lane at a speed of approximately 40 mph.

Foster Brookes Junior pulled up next to George and after Tom counted to three, George and Mr. Smirnoff punched their gas pedals to the floor. The out-come was very similar to the race with Jack's Chevic, which surprised us all. The forty jumped about a half car length ahead and really didn't pull much beyond that, but who knows, maybe he never shifted!

George slowed as we came to the Passaic River bridge, but "Joe

Vodka" and the "Smirnoff Special" disappeared into the night at full throttle never to be seen again in a vision sort of like a scene out of a Henry Gregor Felson novel. Who knows, we could have ended up like this guy if we kept having beer parties, but I doubt it.

That was really about it for George racing the '57 Ford though. Any more racing would have to wait a while until he could afford something with a little more power even though the old Ford gave a pretty good showing. In reality we all knew it was the other two cars that did not live up to what was expected of them! Just goes to show, not everything turns out as it would first appear it should! Just another little lesson in life, of which many seemed to come at us on a regular bases.

We did, however, start going to Island Dragway more frequently now that George had a car. One time while there, we were sitting in the stands on the spectator's side and a highly modified Oldsmobile powered Model A Ford coupe blew a clutch directly in front of us. I actually saw the parts coming towards us and managed to duck down as did my friends. I heard a girl in front of me screaming and crying that she was hit! I looked up at her and she was holding her head, then I saw a clutch pressure plate spring stuck in her hair! I pulled the spring out of her hair and showed it to her! Lucky for her, that was all that hit her! A little scary, but it could have been a lot worse! After that incident I thought, perhaps the spectators should be wearing helmets also!

Chapter Nineteen:
I'll Meet You on Route 21 Right After Temple, and 348s Rule!

No question about it, things were getting busier for us as we grew older and now that George had his car we were at least able to go places without standing around hoping the older guys would ask us to go for a ride. Now our parents started to worry about us being out in a car all the, but it was a lot less dangerous than hitch-hiking as evidenced by the episode with that "numb-nuts" Larry Komar and his attempt at, or fake attempt at suicide, but they were never told of that incident.

The older guys; Danny Bray, Al Marcioni and Fred Schroeder, Vic Monia and others that were now four or more years older than us were now all buying new high-performance, so there was always a race going on that we could go to watch.

At the same time there were quite a number of guys from Passaic and Passaic Park that were also getting new hi-po cars. A large number of these guys were Jewish. The only reason I mention their faith, which made no difference to them or us at all, is that in that era it was fairly common to see these Jewish kids drag racing their cars for money down on Route 21, at the Garden State Parkway ten cents drags, at Grady's in Paterson or anywhere else that street drag races were being held. Today that would be an anomaly.

We would always see them at "Gasoline Alley" in Paterson getting their cars tuned at Dayton Ignition or modified by Roscoe "Pappy" Hough at Hough Motors, or getting their engines "blue-printed" at J & J Balancing or Dick Simonek's.

This (Jewish kids participating in drag racing) was not unusual at all, but today it would be (with the exception of a very small contingent, that is), unheard of to see Jewish kids drag racing, especially on the street, and I'm not sure why that is. Something changed for sure, but I'm not sure what. Maybe the disappearance in general of the middle class, blue collar, skilled worker, Jewish or otherwise.

Anyway, one drag race pitted Danny Bray's black 280 horsepower, 348 cubic inch, three-speed stick shift '61 Chevy Impala sport coupe against one of the Jewish kids 318 horsepower, 389 cubic inch, automatic transmission equipped, Coronado Red '61 Pontiac Bonneville convertible with the name "Jewish Lightning" painted on the lower front fenders.

The Pontiac had more cubic inches and more horsepower, but gave away some in the overall weight department. Both cars had factory three-two barrel carburetor systems and both cars were running Atlas Bucron tires for better traction. I thought that under normal conditions the Pontiac would have a little edge getting off the line, but Danny could drive the Chevy proficiently and could get the Impala "out-of-the-hole" with great consistency.

Al Marcioni was the designated "flag-man." This position was probably as or more dangerous than taking a ride with Larry Komar.

Having a flag-man for this race was decided upon to try and squeeze the slightest bit of an advantage out of using a subtle signal to facilitate an "early warning leave" aptly named the "Delawanna count."

They (Danny, Fred and Al) decided that Danny had to beat this Pontiac, not only for the money, but because the owner was, at times, an extremely arrogant person and they wanted to shut him up as he was already bragging before the race even started.

Both cars entered Route 21 south-bound at the River Road entrance ramp. This was actually the safest place to run on Route 21(if there was such a thing as safe street racing, which there wasn't) as the highway started at that point from the north, so the only cars that could come up behind you were cars that entered from the same ramp they just entered from.

The cars lined up in the slow and middle lane just below Rutt's Hut. Al jumped out of Danny's car leaving Fred still riding with Danny. Al stood about thirty feet in front of the cars and pointed first to Danny with the handkerchief he held in his right hand. Danny with his rpms up to about two-thousand on the steering column mounted Sun tachometer nodded "yes," indicating he was ready. Al then pointed to Pontiac guy receiving a nod that he was also ready. His Pontiac "hunched up" in the rear from the effects of "power-braking" the automatic transmission.

Al lower his "flag-hand" and then, in a split second, just before he raised it again to start the race, he gave Danny the signal by moving his left hand off his knee.

Danny left the line perfectly, as did the Pontiac, but the Pontiac was a split-second late (hmmm) and Danny had a half fender on him. Danny ran the 280 Chevy up to five-thousand rpms and completed the shift to second gear before he fully released the accelerator causing the Chevy to burn the tires in second gear due to the built-up torque created by the partial power-shift. He pulled another half car length on the Poncho after the gear change. Back up to five-thousand rpms and the shift to third found Danny a full car length ahead of the Big Chief. By the time they crossed the finish line, Danny had him by one and one half car lengths. He really didn't need the Delawanna count after all, but you never know...why take a chance?!

These Jewish drag racers hung out in groups of Jewish and non-Jewish kids. They were mostly all blue-collar, middle and upper-middle-class workers. They went through the city school systems of whatever town they lived in and most of them worked in their parents or relatives business'. Almost all of them had the money to buy the "hot" cars.

Most of them had nice cars, such as the aforementioned Pontiac. There were several other high performance Pontiacs within the group of Jewish kids that we knew from Passaic Park among other makes of high performance cars. For example, Howie Bickoff owned a beautiful Nassau Blue, 380 horsepower 409 cubic inch '62 Chevy Super Sport convertible. To this day Howie still owns a '78 Corvette that he purchased brand new and he is still a "regular" at Rutt's Hut cruise nights.

Another one of the Passaic Park Jewish drag racers, Al (Albie) Olster went on to campaign a very successful '63 Plymouth max wedge super stock drag car called "One Step Beyond" followed by another successful Camero race car. He was a very prolific drag-racer and well-known competitor, not just locally, but throughout the N.H.R.A.(National Hot Rod Association)

Back in those days it seemed as though there was at least one race to watch every night, and sometimes more. We started going to all the car hang-outs such as; Rutt's Hutt & Bertlins Grille; Bonds Ice Cream in Styretown; Poppy's on Van Houten Ave. and Richard's Drive-in on Route 46, all of these establishments were located in Clifton. We also frequented The Texan on Route 23, in Wayne; Jif Jiffys on Route 17 in Hasbrouck Heights; The Adventurer Car Hop on Route 22 in Union and so forth and so on hoping there would be a race from one of these hang-outs, and often there was.

One of the worst places to race, in terms of being dangerous, was, in my opinion, Kuller Road in Clifton. It was a desolate one lane stretch of road in an area inhabited only by a few warehouses and factories. It was pretty pitch black there at night with only a few dimly lit street lamps. The reason it was so dangerous was that one of the cars had to be in the on-coming traffic lane! On occasion, whenever a race developed out of Richard's Drive-In, it would be held on Kuller Road. I witnessed several races there, and as bad as that location was for the racers themselves, it was great to observe races there from the neatly manicured lawn of General Foods adjacent to the road itself. It also placed the spectators and their cars off the roadway, which made it somewhat safer for the racers and spectators alike, but it still was an accident waiting to happen.

One night while at Richard's we saw a group of guys talking and then head to their cars, a clear indication of an impending race. Whenever something like that happened, we would just get in line and follow them to whatever location they decided on. This particular night the first two cars, and obvious opponents, to pull out of Richard's, were a Honduras Maroon '61 Chevy Belair Sport Coupe powered by a 348 cubic inch 350 horsepower engine, equipped with a four-speed transmission and owned by a fellow named Vic Tani. Vic was a regular at Richard's and an acquaintance of the older guys from our town. He was followed by a Cashmere Blue and Polo White '55 Chevrolet Belair two-door sedan owned by a guy named Bill Southern. The older guys from Delawanna knew him as well and told us that his car had a 1960 Chevy 348cubic inch 335 horsepower engine and also ran a four-speed transmission.

Should be a pretty even race I thought, even though the '55 was giving a little away in the horsepower department, the '61Belair was giving away about five-hundred pounds in the overall weight department, and that's a lot of weight; It's the equivalent of having three passengers in the car. At least back when we were trim and fit teenagers it was.

Anyway, they made their way to Kuller Road. We pulled into General Foods lot and sat down on the lawn, which was on higher ground and overlooked the road-way giving us spectators a nice view.

The only good thing about Kuller Road from a racing standpoint was that, at the time, it was a very lightly traveled roadway. That being said, we watched the two Chevies go to the far end of Kuller Road near the Hazel Road exit at the Paterson line, turn around and line up facing our direction. One car was on the right side (both literally and figuratively) of the road and the other car on the wrong side of the road.

Just as they were about to go, a car came from the south end traveling north and the race cars had to pull back to the curb to allow the driver that was trying to use the roadway for it's legal, intended purpose to pass by.

Once the car was past the drivers lined up again and we waited with great anticipation for the race to begin, even though we had no favorite in this race. Looking to the north end we could see both sets of headlights raise up and the race was under way. The headlights on the car in the right lane dipped slightly and then jumped back up indicating a shift from first to second gear followed almost immediately by the same reaction from the car in the left lane, neither of which we could identify as a particular car at that time. The headlights of car on the right side dipped again slightly and the jumped back up. The car in the left had a similar reaction a split second later...they were both now in third gear. It appeared by the timing of the car's reactions that the car on the right had a lower ratio rear-end differential causing him to shift a little sooner than the car on the left.

The headlights jumped once more for the forth gear change in the same exact timing sequence. We could then see that the car on the right was Tani's '61 Belair as they came past us and across the finish line at a little over one-hundred miles per hour with the maroon '61 Belair about a fender length ahead. Man, that was a great race from start to finish. Two great cars with two good drivers at the wheel! The difference, after all was said and done, seemed to be in the lower gearing in the '61, which, we learned later was a 4:11to1 compared to the '55's 3;36 to1 ratio rear. I learned a little more about the importance of correctly matched gearing in racing on that night.

Before we got in our cars to leave someone told us to wait as another race was to take place there in a very short time. We all went back to the lawn to wait and within thirty minutes or so we saw a burgundy colored 1940 Ford Deluxe coupe pass by with the odd name of "Bazz Buzz" painted on the fenders. My first thought was; Oh Christ, is this Mr. Smirnoff? If it was, I could understand the "Buzz" part of the name! Then one of the other guys watching with us told us that Bazz Buzz was owned by a guy named George King and that it was Oldsmobile powered. I remembered his name from school and George said he knew him and had him in several of his classes, but he knew nothing about the Forty Ford he was driving. The car following Bazz Buzz was Bill Southern in the blue and white '55 Belair again. This time it was the '55 Chevy giving away a three-hundred plus pound weight advantage to the little Forty with the 371 cubic inch Oldsmobile J-2 engine, which also had a cubic inch edge, but needed thirty-five more horses to match the Chevy.

This time when the cars drove to the end and turned around I could tell which car was which due to the headlights being closer together on the '40 coupe. When the car's front ends lifted under power at the start of the race I could see that the Forty got "out of shape" a little from an obvious loss of traction at the starting line. The '55 was clearly out in front and I could see it's front end jumping up and down during the power-shifts to higher and higher gears. They came past us again at the finish line, but this time the '55 was out in front by two full car lengths. It appeared the Forty lost the race right out of the hole when it lost traction. That's all it takes; It's hard to make up a car length or more unless your car completely over-powers the other car. It was another fun race to watch, and hearing the tri-power singing in that little factory colored '55 in the crisp night air as well as that of the triple Rochesters on the J-2 Olds powered Forty was an inspiring sound for any gear-head…of which I was one!

Chapter Twenty:
New Cars for Some but Not All

Joe Mattiello would be the next one in our group to get his driver's license and he was sure of what car he wanted to get. It would be a brand new '62 Chevy Super Sport. He decided on that particular car because he saw George's new '62 Impala when George took delivery in September of 1961. George, however, had no idea what the '62 Chevies were going to look like when he ordered his in the summer of 1961. That's the way it was back then. You couldn't see the new cars until the unveiling date at the dealership; Just lots of speculation as to what they might look like. The new cars were delivered completely covered and they stayed that way until that special day which was hyped in the newspapers and on television. If you had a new car on order or you were a preferred customer would get a special pre-unveiling peek at the new cars, otherwise you had to wait to see them like everyone else. We used to drive around to all the dealers to look at the clandestine white covered shapes parked as far out of sight as they could put them on their lots. We would then try to figure out what they looked like, which was next to impossible, but it was fun and exciting to try.

George ordered his Chevy sight unseen after he found out that Ford Motor Company did not plan on building a Starliner for the 1962 year line-up. That news turned him off on a Ford purchase and sent him over to G.M. His logic was that if the '62 Chevies looked anything like the '61 Chevies, he would be happy. Well, they didn't look anything at all like a '61, but George was very happy with they way they did look just the same, and so was Joe, so that clinched it for him; A'62 Chevy it would be!

George's '62 was a straight Impala 327 cubic inch 300 horsepower car with a three-speed standard transmission. Joe ordered an Impala Super Sport equipped with the same 327/300 and three-speed transmission combination as George's car. Joe's car was ordered in Nassau Blue with matching blue bucket seat interior and George's car was all black with red interior and a red strip inside the aluminum side molding.

Now that Joe also had his license, and a new Chevy, we were always going somewhere. The cars opened up a whole new world of freedom to us. At a moments notice we would go anywhere we felt like going. We would, at times, go over to Palisades Amusement Park, which was only one half hour away, on Saturday nights to see the Clay Cole Show, but usually we wound up back at one of the car cruise joints in the local area hoping to see a drag race.

It didn't matter which one of these cruise places you chose to go to, they were all filled with hot cars whose owners were just itching for a drag race. Unless it was raining or snowing, it was a safe bet you were going to see someone race.

It was 1962 and the "big three" automobile manufacturers; Ford, G.M. and Chrysler had all pushed their high performance engine options to over four-hundred cubic inches. You couldn't pull into one of these cruise spots without seeing at least one or two cars of the factory super stock variety there along with numerous other lower stock class and medium performance cars such as Joe's and George's 327s. But still, at that time, there was an abundance of the highly modified older model cars like Bill Southern's '55 Chevy and the Bazz Buzz forty coupe than there were the high performance factory cars; Mainly due to the initial cost I would suspect. It was way less expensive to buy, say a clean '55 Chevy for two to three hundred dollars and then look for or build a high performance motor to drop in, than it was to purchase a factory hi-po car for twenty seven hundred to three thousand dollars.

Older Chevies and Fords were the favorites to modify, with Chevy probably being the easiest with regards to parts and adaptability of other engines from G.M.s vast line-up of hi-po and easily modified small blocks. Older Fords were a little harder even though a big bock "FE" would bolt into a '54 and up chassis, but there was limited room for exhaust headers, which were essential.

Older Ford coupes like Bazz Buzz and the Smirnoff Special could be had for next to nothing. It was not difficult at all to find a '40 Ford coupe to modify for fifty bucks or so.

The only problem with this type of car was the straight axle factory front ends they used were usually completely worn out by the time the hot rodders got their hands on them and only the most diligent of these youthful racers would bother to get the front end, brake and steering in shape before any speed modifications took place. Also, some of the modifications necessary to install a bigger engine and transmission in these cars required splitting the wishbones or some other suspension modifications that would affect the front end geometry in a negative way. After-all, the object was to get the car to go fast, so little regard was given to safety in some cases. This made for a number of overpowered, ill-handling pre-1948 hot rods! (Sort of like my bicycle-built-for-two project with Jimmy Walsh, but with greater consequences at stake).

Most of these highly modified older cars could not make it through the New Jersey State Motor Vehicle inspection that was required to legally operate any car on New Jersey roads. The resultant hassle of being pulled over and ticketed by the police for no validated inspection made it stressful on the owner's of these cars. They were always sneaking around, trying to avoid the police. This pushed a lot of guys into buying the newer factory high performance cars. At least they would or should pass inspection most of the time, but they didn't pass all of the time. There were times when a brand new hi-po car would fail for loud exhaust or from having the front-end raised up (a common practice in the early to mid 1960s). Fred Schroeder was stopped in Totowa by a State Police officer and issued a loud exhaust summons in his brand new 1962 Ford Galaxie two-door sedan equipped with the 406 cubic inch, 405 horsepower engine option on the first week he owned the car! The car wasn't loud at all as it had an unmodified factory exhaust system. It was a little lopey as most hi-po cars were due to the lift and duration of the factory camshaft. The State Trooper didn't want to hear anything about cams durations, lifts or whatever. He said that is his opinion it was too loud, so he issued Fred a summons! The car did, however, pass N.J. inspection, which was tough to do with the older modified cars.

The city of Clifton and it's neighboring towns were starting to fill up with high-performance cars. You couldn't go anywhere without seeing young guys and their high performance "factory hot rods" or highly modified older cars. They were all over. And so were the street drag races.

Danny Bray was a little concerned at the amount of the, still unproven, 327/300 Chevies sprouting up all over as they would probably be in his class using the horsepower to weight calculations. Eventually, after racing George, Joe and several other similarly equipped '62s, he realized that the little 280 horse '61 could put most of them "on the trailer" and he regained confidence in his '61 Chevy.

With the time approaching rapidly for me to join the ranks of the licensed drivers of New Jersey I had to focus on what I was going to get as my first legal street car. So, after seeing and admiring all the high performance late model Fords, Chevies, Pontiacs and Chrysler products in Delawanna and the surrounding towns, and after much thought and consideration, I decided I had to have…a 1954 Oldsmobile Ninety Eight four-door sedan. Yep…that was the car for me! I'm kidding of course…not about getting the Olds, which I actually did get, but about wanting it! As I said before, I hope it was a matter of pure economics, otherwise I definitely had a very low opinion of myself!

Back then a new hi-po Ford or Chevy was twenty-seven hundred plus dollars and I had…sixty-five dollars! Actually, I had fifty dollars and had to borrow fifteen dollars from my father, plus enough to cover registration fees and a down-payment of twenty-five dollars for the one-hundred and twenty-five dollar insurance premium, The remainder I could pay off on a monthly basis. Back then you could also apply for N.J. State insurance for a fifty dollar annual premium, but I was reluctant to do so because, neither myself or anyone else I asked about it fully understood what it was all about.

My friends and I did have some fun in that old '54 Olds (named "The Duke"), but we just didn't really want to be seen in it. It was really a very un-cool car and the only thing even remotely cool about it was the 324 cubic inch Rocket Eighty Eight engine that resided under the massive green hood just screaming to be taken out and be put into a lighter Ford or Chevy body. Great motor, bad car…for a seventeen year old kid that is. But, it got me on the road regardless of what it was for the time being.

We used to take The Duke to Wetson's or Goody's drive-in hamburger restaurants on Route 46 in Little falls and West Paterson. Both of these places were similar to a Mc Donald's and we used to frequent them to feed our youthful appetites. They were both places I could take the Olds and not be embarrassed, as they were not car hang-outs, so my car fit in with all the "family type" cars that could be found there. Another benefit of taking The Duke to these places was we that didn't have to worry about getting any condiments on the seats like we would have if we used George or Joe's cars. What's a little ketchup or mayonnaise on an already stained seat upholstery. That one six inch in diameter stain in the driver's seat of the Olds always bothered me though when I considered what age group the original owner was most likely from. Actually, he probably came from the same age group that I am part of as of this writing! Now that I think of it, my worst fears are confirmed! Time to change the subject.

We would also take The Duke to the Melody Hill Diner on Route 46 west-bound in Clifton directly across the street from Bowlero Bowling Alley. We would often times meet some of the guys we went to school with there and hang-out talking cars with them. We got along with most of them, but there was always that "protecting your turf" thing if it came to any of us showing interest in any of the girls from their side of town, the same way it was with us if they came to Delawanna. It wasn't a big deal, just that territorial thing that most guys have. It must be a primal instinctive reaction that is beyond our control. Besides, if we went anywhere to look for girls, we wouldn't have taken The Duke unless we were trying to impress some girl's grandparents!

The guys that hung-out at the Melody Diner weren't as "into" the high-performance cars as the Delawanna and Allwood guys were. Some of them had nice cars, but very few of them were high-performance. I should talk, my Olds not only wasn't high-performance, it wasn't even a nice car! The only reason I felt even the slightest bit comfortable with bringing the Olds there was that Pete Pach used to go there often with his super, quadruple, double throw-down, absolute numero uno in the winner of the "ugly-as-a-bag-of-assholes" contest…'51 Chrysler…appropriately named, "The Possum"! (A great insult to the comparative good looks of an actual Possum, I might add!)

Also, Al Hamilton, whom we attended school with and who was a regular at the Melody Hill Diner, owned a two-tone Emerald and Satin Green visually challenged '55 Dodge four-door sedan that rivaled The Dukes "designed for senior citizen looks," only it was seven-hundred pounds lighter, possibly making it a high-performance car by comparison. So, The Duke was in good company most of the time at the Melody Hill Diner. All three of these aforementioned cars were good examples of bad examples in terms of what a seventeen year old male should be driving if he wanted to be the least bit cool, but it was the best some of us could do at the time.

Our diner hang-out was the Tick Tock Diner on Route 3 west in the Allwood section of Clifton, which bordered Delawanna. We would stop there every night for a cup of coffee before we went home and also to ogle at the very good looking (but way too old for us at twenty-six years of age) divorced waitress, Annie. She would often sit with us and talk, as long as the Surrey Lane boys didn't come in. If they did show up, then she had to be on guard, because some of them had a habit of ripping off a piece of the turkey that sat on the counter whenever no one was looking among other things that use to piss off her and Nick, the owner.

The Surrey Lane guys, of which there were seven or eight, all had high-performance cars. We knew them all well from school and shared in their car interest, which was our common bond to them. Surrey Lane itself looked like the starting line at Island Dragway with all the black strips on the road surface. It must have been hell on the neighbors as I think if it now! Possibly more on these guys later. First I have to make sure all statutes of limitations have run out on any "alleged" incidents they might have or might not have been involved in.

Chapter Twenty-One:
The '57 Ford That was Not to Be and the Cajun Queen!

In the summer 1962 I needed to do something about my ownership of the land yacht of a car I was driving. I was starting to feel like one of the kids that didn't make the team and was sent home crying, as a social castoff, from Little League try-outs. This car was definitely hurting the image that I wanted, but didn't have yet, and if and when I did get one (an image that is) I didn't want this car being attached to any part of it. So, it was time to relinquish command of this vessel of low self esteem and hand over the wheel, and all stains, to another, more appreciative captain. Then I would, in turn, get a car that would be somewhat cool at the very least.

As I stated in Hot Rods, Pink-bellies and Hank Ballard, my next car was a 1956 Ford Customline two-door hardtop that I purchased from Fred Schroeder after he bought a new '62 406 Ford. I bought the '56 with a bad '54 Mercury engine in it. Actually the description of a "bad '54 Mercury engine" is an oxymoron, because, in my opinion, at least back then, if you had any '54 Mercury engine, old or new, you had a bad engine!

Anyhow, I now had a cool car, but a useless, tired and under-powered engine. Just the opposite from the Olds, which had a great engine, but the car was way…un-cool. Between these cars I had the makings of a nice hot rod, just not at the same time. This would not be the last time this scenario would affect me in regards to not having all the hot rod stars lined up.

Most of the trials and tribulations of this car were documented in my earlier book, so I won't go into all that again. It did take me where I wanted to go and I wasn't embarrassed taking it to car hang-outs. I just couldn't really race it, even though I replaced the tired old Merc with a "seen better days" 292 cubic inch Y block. I mean, if I could have found Jack Jorg and his Chevick I think I would have stood a chance, but he didn't come around much anymore. He was an old man by then; At least twenty-seven years old!

The '56 Ford was fairly dependable, but was hard to start on cold mornings. There were times when the temperature dipped that it would not fire at all. When that occurred I would have to spay some starting fluid in the carburetor and have my mother push me down the street, so I wouldn't be late for my job at Arrow Carrier in Carlstadt, N.J. I used to worry that she would break an arm when I jumped in, put it in gear and "popped" the clutch, But she was a tough old Canadian farm girl and was used to much worse. Just the same, I didn't need anyone seeing her having to push me down the street at 7am.

One Wednesday night we took a ride to the "lemon groves" (that was the name we gave to the strip of numerous used car lots on Route 46 in Little Ferry, N.J.) While there I spotted an all white '57 Ford Fairlane two-door hardtop that had a 312 cubic inch 245 horsepower Thunderbird special V/8 with a four-barrel carburetor and a three-speed overdrive transmission. They were asking five-hundred and fifty dollars for the car and by the time we left, I had myself convinced that I was going to own this car. It was a pretty rare car in that it was a Fairlane two-door hardtop and not a Fairlane 500. You didn't see many of them and they were much more subtle and clean looking than the 500 model, in my opinion.

Anyway, all the way home we talked about this car and my plan to get my father to co-sign for a loan so I could buy it. But that all changed in a quick moment when I was stopped by "Red," the notorious teenage hating Wallington, N.J. cop for speeding. I tried to tell him that I wasn't going more than thirty miles an hour, but he gave me a ticket for fifty-five in a twenty-five and said, "Tough shit sonny, tell it to the judge" He didn't use radar, he didn't even pace me. He just saw me go past and heard the slightly load exhaust (leaking through the flex-pipe temporary exhaust that I never got around to replacing) and decided I was going fifty-five!

That was it for the co-signing. There was no way my father would sign for the loan with this pending ticket; Especially considering it was for speeding! So the prospects of owning the '57 disappeared along with the money for lawyer fees after my father insisted I get a lawyer friend of his to go to court with me. All that did was add to my cost, because once we got to court, he said there wasn't much he could do. Actually, the best thing he could have done for me was to stay home; At least I wouldn't have had to pay him for doing absolutely nothing!

It was one step forward and two steps back in my attempts to climb the high performance ladder, but at least I didn't have that Olds anymore. On second thought, if I did still have the Olds, I'll bet that bastard Red wouldn't have stopped me at all. He would have never considered that a teenager boy would have been behind the wheel of that General Motors senior citizen taxi!

Friday night came along and the speeding ticket incident was pushed to back of my thoughts for the time being, so we all headed to Bonds in Styretown, because we heard there was to be a big race between a '62 409 Chevy Belair Sport Coupe from Pequanock, owned by a guy named Billy Aires. My friends and I had never heard of him before, but Danny, Al, Fred and Joe Alterizio knew him from going to The Texan on Route 23 for the past few years.

Bond's parking lot started to fill up early that night there. It appeared that everyone else had also heard of this up-coming race. Within a half hour or so about eight cars pulled in together. Some of them I recognized, like the Honduras Maroon '61 Biscayne with the name "Bisquick" on the lower front fenders and the nearly identical Biscayne named "Watusi." Both cars had the 348 cubic inch 350 horse option with four-speed transmissions.

The procession was led by a car I had never seen before, but I knew from pre-race information that it was, in fact, Billy Aires in his '62 Chevy Belair 409 Sport Coupe two-door hardtop. The car was very distinguishable from any of the other cars there, or anywhere else for that matter, at least as far as I was concerned. It was the absolute ultimate street racing super stock car that my friends and I had seen to date, outside of the race track that is.

It was only the second 409 Belair Sport Coupe I'd ever seen. The first one was "The Buzzard," a highly competitive regular race car at Island Dragway. The Belair Sport Coupe body style was pretty rare, even back then, with it's up-dated '62 body style, all the while retaining the 1961 Chevy "bubble top" roof. It really made for a beautiful combination and looked like it was going a hundred miles per hour even as it sat standing still.

Once Billy and his friends parked their cars, they walked over to talk to the older guys from Delawanna. My friends and I then walked over to look at the Ermine White Belair with the red interior, black wall tires with no hub caps on the factory white wheels and the name "Cajun Queen" painted down almost the full length of both sides of the car. This, I thought, had to be the coolest name ever for a car, possibly rivaled only by Don Garlit's "The Swamp Rat"

The intimidating looking Cajun Queen sat there with the nose of the car raised up considerably higher than stock. It had a pair of Casler "cheater slicks" mounted on the rear wheels and header "dumps" running down the outside of the front fender wells, exciting between the tire and the lower part of the front fender. Near the forward part of the front fenders was the familiar crossed flags that both George and Joe's '62s had, as did all 1962 Chevies equipped with 327 cubic inch engines. On this car, however, in chrome block form figures, were the numbers "409" underneath the crossed flags, indicating this car was equipped with Chevrolet's "serious" high-performance "W" style motor, of which there was a single four-barrel carburetor 380 horse power version and a dual four-barrel carburetor 409 horsepower version available from the G.M. factory.

When Billy opened the hood to show the older guys the engine it became obvious to me that this particular 409 was of the higher horse power version. Other distinctive modifications were also apparent at that time such as; the Spaulding Flame-thrower ignition and the very noticeable Jardine fender-well headers. This car was pretty serious and we were completely impressed to say the least.

After some discussion we learned from one of the guys that Billy's opponent for the race was a highly modified '61 Corvette from Union, N.J. (about twenty-five miles south/west of us) and they were to meet up with this guy at the Adventurer Car Hop on Route 22. The race was going to be for one-hundred dollars, which was a lot of money back then when most people didn't make that in a week; I know I certainly didn't and neither did any of my friends. The reason he came to Bonds was to have as much support with him as possible considering the fact he was racing out of town and really didn't know any of the guys from the Adventurer

As everybody headed for their cars, Ted, Ronnie and I hoped in George's car and Tom, Swissy and Phil hoped in Joe's '62. As we followed the procession out of Bond's lot, we were directly behind Bobby Ward's black '59 270 horsepower Corvette. We drove up Route 3 west to the Garden State Parkway south-bound with Aire's white Belair in the lead. When we pulled onto the Parkway, he stopped the Belair in the slow lane, bought up the rpms and pulled a "hole shot." The car "left" very hard with the Casler's biting into the concrete road surface just as they were intended to. It was also obvious at this time that the car had, at the very least, a 4:56 or 4:88 rear end gear ratio as the gear change to second came very soon after the initial "launch." This car was very impressive indeed!

We continued south and excited onto Route 22 west and stayed on that roadway for the remainder of the trip to the Adventurer Car Hop. This would be the first time my friends and I were going there and we were excited at the prospects of watching the Cajun Queen race. But, our excitement was to be short lived.

We followed the line of cars into the famous hamburger establishment and the first thing I noticed was that the Adventurer's lot was full of police cars. There were cops all over the lot with very few kids hanging out and no high-performance car sightings at all. The first cop we came across appeared to be a high ranking officer, either a captain or at least a lieutenant. He walked over to Billy Aires and said in a very gruff voice filled with contempt, "Get that f--kin' Cajun Queen the Hell out of here and stay out!" "And the same goes for the rest of you asshole drag racing smart-asses!" Not sure where the smart-ass comment came from as no one said anything at all to him. It was a good the Frank Miner (I wrote about him in the last book) wasn't there with us or there would have been a problem for sure as he always wanted the last say with the police no matter if he was right or wrong. And he/we were almost always wrong or the police wouldn't be there in the first place! Duh!

Sometimes, in spite of all of the effort, things ended up like this for us back then. Somehow they (the police) had been pre-warned of the up-coming race and put the "kibosh" on it this time. Oh well, that's the way it goes. I mean, what recourse did we have? What were we going to say, "Ah come-on, you're kidding right captain, no race…and after we drove all the way down here!"

Well, we all left the Adventurer and headed back to the welcome familiarity of our home town and the Bond's parking lot. Billy Aires just honked the Cajun Queen's horn, waved and kept going as we turned off Route 3 west at the Bloomfield Ave. exit. I never saw that car again, but I will never forget it. It left an lasting impression on me, even though I never actually saw it race. It was just one of those cars that had a powerful, almost human presence, if you know what I mean. Way, way too cool for words!

Chapter Twenty-Two:
Fifty-Sick Chevy

I could see the blue nose of what I recognized to be a '56 Chevy sitting in one of the bays at the "Little Beaver Gas and Used Car Lot" on Hazel Road in Clifton, near the Paterson border on a cool March evening in 1963. As I waited for my usual buck-fifty worth of gas I asked the attendant, "What's the story with the '56 Chevy?" He said it was going to go on the lot for sale as soon as they finished rebuilding the engine. I turned to Ronnie and Ted, my passengers at the time and said, "What do you think, wanna take a look?" They both agreed that we should.

After getting approximately five gallons of gas I pulled my black and white '56 Ford to the opposite side of the lot and we walked back to the bay to check out the '56, which, as we got closer and could see more of the car, turned out to be a Belair convertible. The hood was opened and it had a red, newly painted engine installed but the job wasn't completed as of yet. The car was two-toned in a nice shade of blue and white that I later found to be the original G.M. colors of Nassau Blue and India Ivory. It had a white top, full hub caps, was nosed and decked with a custom tube grille.

The mechanic was in the rear of the bay cleaning the valve covers, which had yet to be installed. I asked him how much they were asking for the car and when he turned around to say he wasn't sure, I, at first, thought it was George the mechanic from Delawanna Building Supply; he was the spitting image of him and could easily have been his brother. I then saw the name "Jim" on his Little Beaver work shirt and hoped it was his shirt and not a borrowed one. So, before proceeding any further with this car, I asked him if he happened to have a brother named George, to which he advised me that he didn't. Then, trying to be funny for the sake of my friends, I asked, "So, do you use any sand during the course of rebuilding an engine?" He gave me a very confused look and said, "Why the hell would anyone use sand during the rebuilding of an engine?" I took that as a rhetorical question, but as this whole thing played out, maybe I shouldn't have.

Anyway the Little Beaver owner, a short, fat guy in his mid to late thirties came in and said, "So, you guys interested in this Chevy?" Without waiting for an answer he went on to tell us of all it's attributes such as; the rebuilt engine that hadn't even been run yet. He empathized the word *even*. Now, I know he meant that as a positive thing, but to me, the fact that it hadn't been run yet did not make the "happy meter" jump up at all. After all, I witnessed George the mechanic's engine rebuild and believe me, everything was fine before he tried to "run" it! As a matter of fact, it looked like he did a good job. Everything was clean, and from a visual stand-point, it looked like it would run fine, just like this one did. Only it didn't! So, so much for the "it hasn't *even* been run yet statement"!

The owner told me to come back in two days and it should be running. So, two days later I showed up with Ted, Ronnie and Swissy in tow and when I pulled in I saw the '56 sitting outside of the bay with the hood back on, so I figured it must be finished. I talked to the owner and he said that, in fact, it was "ready to go." Another term that can be taken more than one way. It can mean it's all done and you can go anywhere with the car with confidence or, when I think back nine years prior, to the day the doctor came to my house to check my aging, sickly grandmother it takes on a different meaning. After checking my grandmother, the doctor motioned with his head to my father to go to the next room where I overheard him say, "It appears that she's…*ready to go.*" Two days later dear old Granny was gone!

Trying to be positive, (that was getting harder and harder to do as I got older and met more and more adults who were supposed to be mature and dependable but, in my opinion, were totally inept and often…full of shit) I followed him to the car and he started it up. I'll have to say, it did sound pretty good. I opened the hood and checked for any tell-tale signs of sand or evidence of fire, but there was none…to be seen that is!

After a test drive, I decided that I really liked this car. I mean I wasn't crazy about the automatic transmission, but I thought I could always change it to stick. I also wasn't sure how I would like a convertible. You know, driving around with the top down for all the world to see you. I thought maybe that part of it wouldn't be for me, but it sure was a nice looking car and after some negotiating he came down to four hundred and seventy-five dollars and said he would give me fifty dollars for my Ford and a *fifty-fifty* warranty. I wasn't too sure how the fifty-fifty warrantee worked, without thinking much further, I said "OK" and gave him a ten dollar deposit.

I picked the Chevy up the following week after I got an auto loan with monthly payments that I needed like I needed a pair of sixty-grit sand-paper underwear. Initially, when I went to start the car, it seemed to turn-over a little slow, which gave me great concern. The mechanic, Jim, said, "It's a little tight because it's new. It will take a while for it to break in." That wasn't reassuring at all to me, because it reminded me of George's "tight" engine rebuild.

After it started, I pulled away from the lot and took a long, hard look at my '56 Ford sitting there looking forlorn (if a car can actually look that way). I actually felt like I was leaving my best friend behind. This whole thing was supposed to feel great, but I had this slight feeling of depression instead. Was it buyer's remorse? Was I sad leaving my old Ford there in the hands of…who knows, or was it simply because the mechanic that rebuilt the engine looked so much like George from Delawanna Building Supply? Goddamn it!…I know that's his brother, I thought.

I also had sort of negative feeling, that I can't explain, about driving away in such a pretty car. The old Ford was ratty by comparison, but I think maybe it was more me than a powdery blue convertible, somewhat of a titwillow's type of car. One more negative thing that I never gave even the slightest bit of consideration to was that Larry Komar (suicidal Larry) had an almost identical '56 Chevy at the time. The only difference was that his '56 had a blue top whereas mine was white. Now that small detail is something I shouldn't have had to consider at all when I purchased this car, but the fact that it looked like Larry's car gave me some grief from time to time.

In example of this I offer the time Ronnie, Ted and I were driving down Cherry Street heading to George Harding's house when a middle-aged women in a house coat ran out in the street right in front of me, causing me to slam my brakes on. She starting screaming hysterically at me. She ran over to my window and yelled, "You f--ckin' (she really was pissed, because not many woman used the "F" word back then) son-of-a-bitch, I'll ring your Goddamn neck if you ever come through here again. I'm sick and tired of you racing up and down this street!." She was so pissed off and screaming at me that I couldn't get a word in. Finally I told her it wasn't me, it had to be Larry Komar. She replied, "Oh it was you alright, don't try to tell me any different, I know this Goddamn car!" I then asked her what color the roof was on the car in question and she said, "How the hell do I know?" I was finally able to calm her down by pointing out the difference in the two cars and advised her to look at the roof color the next time. "What if the tops down?," she replied. I said, "Well then try looking at the driver"…duh! There were several other mix-ups with people confusing my car with his during my '56 Chevy ownership and none of the were due to anything positive.

One night while driving through Wallington with Ted and George in the '56 with the top down, we stopped alongside two girls that were walking down Paterson Ave. and asked them if they needed wanted a ride. Actually, we weren't really concerned if they actually needed a ride, we only hoped they did because we needed / wanted girls, any girls! They said they didn't really need a ride, but that they would like to go for one and then, without any hesitation, climbed in the back seat with the three of us still in the front. This was working out pretty well so far, except for the three of us still seated in the front. They got in the car so fast I started to think, maybe this convertible was a good idea after-all.

These girls, as it turned out, were a little wilder, make that a lot wilder than the girls we were used to. The one girl sat up on the seat back and started yelling at people on the street. Then Ted says to me, "She just picked up her sweater and flashed those guys we just passed!" Within a few moments he says, "She did it again!" All this was great, except by me being the driver I did not witness any of this, and was, without a doubt, wishing that I did. After we passed another group Ted leans over and says; "She's doing it again!" This time I replied, "Unless you are ready to drive, please do not tell me that again!"

At the light at Paterson Ave. and Park Ave. some guy calls to the girls by name prompting them both to jumped out of the Chevy and say, "Thanks for the ride," they then walked away with that guy and two or three others that were with him there-by slamming the brakes on any salacious thoughts any of us might have had; Especially after the exhibition the one girl put for all (except me) to see.

Well anyway, Easter Sunday, April 14th 1963 was a beautiful day to have a convertible, and I just happened to have one on that day. I was driving down Ridge Road in North Arlington with Ronnie, Ted, Phil, Darlene and Eileen (Juggy's sister). I had the top down and the mild spring-time air was blowing through our hair and the car running absolutely perfect. Then, without the slightest warning came a horrible metallic clanging noise that sounded as if someone was under the car with a hammer. This noise was followed by a huge plume of smoke coming from under the car. I quickly steered the Chevy to the side of the road and, through the rearview mirror I saw a stream of oil on the road surface trailing the car. We looked under the car and saw oil dripping from puncture holes in the oil pan. These holes were obviously caused by something on the inside of the engine trying to get out! It looked to me like the *"tight new engine"* finally broke in, with *"broke"* being the operative word here!!

That was the end to a perfect Easter Sunday for sure and it appeared as though I was now going to find out exactly how the fifty-fifty warranty worked!

Well, the Chevy was towed to Little Beaver the next day and the first thing I did when I got there was look around to see if my Ford was still there, which sadly, it wasn't. The mechanic, Jim, came over, looked at it and said, "Wow, what did you do to this poor car?" That response from him pissed me off, so I said to him, "I drove it, why was that something your rebuild wasn't up to?!" "It looks like your master rebuild job finally broke in George!" "Calm down, calm down," he says, "let's have a look at it, and my name is Jim." I said, "Yeah, I'll just bet it is!" I added, "If you want to look at it, you'll have to go over to Ridge Road in Lyndhurst, because that's where most of it is!"

It wouldn't have bothered my all that much if I was beating on this car, but I never did abuse it. After all, I certainly wasn't going to race this 265 cubic inch engine with a two-barrel carburetor and a crumby power-glide transmission. The Chevy was really a slug, but I had plans of putting in a 327 and a four-speed someday, although I almost knew in my heart that I would never have the money to make that happen. At this point, I was sorry I didn't just take the four-hundred plus dollars and put it into the Ford!

After the engine was repaired with another complete rebuild consisting of a new crankshaft and one connecting rod, I was back on the road, albeit with even less enthusiasm for this particular car. Also negotiating the fifty-fifty warranty was a stressful experience. At first the lot owner wanted to charge me two-hundred and fifty dollars, so I told him to take the shitty motor back out and I would take the car less engine! I figured for two-hundred and fifty dollars I could buy a used 348 or maybe even a 409, but I certainly wasn't paying two-hundred and fifty dollars for a shitty, under-powered, rebuilt 265. We finally negotiated down to one-hundred dollars, which I still wasn't happy with, but I paid it to get on the road.

The car never felt good to me after that. Actually, I never really felt comfortable with that car to start with. I realized then that I was a cheap-model sedan type of guy, not a powder blue convertible guy. Me in that convertible was like putting a silk tie on a pig, and I finally realized it.

One more incident and that was enough of this car for me. And that happened one night when Eddie Kovatch and I met two girls and made plans to go on a "double-date" with them the following Saturday night. The Chevy was giving me starting trouble when it got hot (still a little tight I guess!) and I was afraid of breaking down while out on this date; You know, actually breaking down, not the phony break-downs guys used to pull from time to time with their dates.

Anyway, Joe Mattiello, after learning of the planned double date, offered to let me use his '62 Chevy Super Sport and said he would take my Chevy for the night. How could I not accept his generous offer? So, we exchanged cars the night of the date and Eddie and I picked up the girls in Joe's fairly new and dependable '62, which Joe cleaned to perfection for us earlier in the day. The girls were impressed by this car to say the least as we picked them up and took them to the Totowa Drive-in Theater on Union Blvd. and Rt.46 in Totowa.

After the show decided to go to the Tick Tock Diner for something to eat. On the way down Allwood Road I spotted my Chevy sitting at the intersection of Market Street and Allwood Road. It appeared as though someone was inside the car, so I did a flip around at the Alwood Circle and pulled up behind the Chevy to find Joe sitting there...broke down! I felt bad that Joe got stuck in my car and we were using his car, but he told me not to worry about it, he would wait for the car to cool down and then try to get back home, which, as I found out later that night, he was able to do.

The following week, I traded the Chevy for a Titian Red '56 Ford Customline two-door sedan with a dented right rear quarter panel plus some money. It really wasn't enough money though, but I made the deal anyway, because this Ford had a perfect running 272 cubic inch V/8 and a three-speed transmission with a Fox Craft floor mounted stick shift. What was even better was that this car fit me and in spite of losing some money, it felt better owning it, and an added bonus was that Larry Komar didn't own one like it!

Chapter Twenty-Three:
Saved by a Hair, Four-Wheeled Coffins and a Memorable Chevy

Well, the new (to me) '56 ford didn't do much for my high-performance desires, but I did feel better about owning it than I did with the '56 Chevy, for whatever odd, sub-conscious reason that was, and still is, I might add. I still prefer cheap-model high-performance or understated cars more than higher-end models or flashy cars.

Although this Ford was far from my dream car, I wasn't the only one that didn't have the funds to buy what I really wanted. There were plenty of kids driving crap way worse than mine. A case in point was Tommy Dione's '55 Pontiac convertible which had to be on the "Junk Yards of America's Most Wanted List." This car was in such poor condition that if he stopped too long at a traffic light, buzzards would start circling over-head! The one and only attribute this car had (to Tommy, that is) was that it was a convertible. Actually, there really wasn't much of a top left on it at all; Mainly just top bows with some evidence of canvas still clinging to them. The bows themselves were in great shape though!

Now that I think of it, Tommy's car didn't really qualify as a convertible, because the word convertible would imply that the top could be put up for protection from the elements. The only thing accomplished by putting Tommy's top up was you could get a stripped sun-burn!

Anyway, one day while I was working at O'Chippa's garage, Tommy and Ted pulled in with this raggedy-assed piece-of-shit and Tommy said, "Hey Bob, take a look at my left front wheel, something is screwed-up." I walked over to the car and saw the left front wheel kicked way out at the bottom to the point where it looked like the car was going to fall on the ground. I told Tommy I would get a jack and lift it up to determine what the problem was. Pontiac suspension, although they used an "A" frame similar to other cars, had a king-pin arrangement rather than a ball-joint and I thought it was likely a badly worn-out king-pin that was the cause of this current situation.

Tommy then got on his side and put his head under the car to further inspect the problem. I told him that he had better get his head out from under the car until we found out exactly what was wrong. Then in the same instant that he pulled his head out from under the car, the king-pin broke and the car slammed to the ground! The bumper crashed right smack-down on the pavement! It missed crushing his head by a fraction of a second! Tommy said he felt the bumper graze his hair!

After our initial shock we all started to laugh. That reaction seemed to be common after a near tragedy such as this. I think it is the body's way to reduce the instantaneous stress caused by a near-death experience, but what the hell do I know. I do and did however, know about Pontiac king-pins and so now does Tommy Dione!

Most kids tried to buy "up" when they purchased another car. I think my '56 Chevy to '56 Ford change was a somewhat questionable move, all things considered, but Tommy's next purchase, as hard as it was to believe, was down several rungs on the ladder from his Pontiac convertible. I didn't think there was a drivable car that was in worse condition than that Pontiac, but Tommy managed to find one! And another convertible at that! This one was a '51 Ford with the shittiest blue paint job I had / have ever seen on a car! It looked like someone applied the paint with a rock! They painted right over the rust and dents and it appeared to be over the dirt too!

This car was so bad that Tommy had the name "Lil' Ridiculous" painted of the front fenders. I would have chosen something a little different if it were mine, which thank God Almighty, it wasn't. However, the amount of expletives I would have used in giving that car a fitting and deserving name would not have fit on the fender! Possibly not even on the whole side of the car!

This Ford actually had a complete canvas top, which the Pontiac didn't, enabling Tom to use the car in inclement weather. That was the only edge it had on the Pontiac. That, and unlike the Pontiac, it hadn't tried to kill him…yet! The only problem was the Ford would not start in inclement weather there-by negating any good that might have been gained from having a top!

Another piece-of-dog-shit on wheels was owned by a guy named John Wry. His choice of a car was a '55 Oldsmobile Ninety Eight two-door hardtop. Now quite often when you would find an upscale car like an Olds, it was usually in pretty decent shape, because it was normally purchased new by an adult of some means. These cars usually didn't get down to the hot rodders until they were quite a bit older than the Chevys or the Fords were. Plus most kids wanted a Chevy or Ford and usually only bought an Olds or Pontiac because of finances. I say all this because John's Olds did not fit the normal used Olds or Pontiac that made it down to our ranks. To put it mildly, John's Olds had all the appeal of a rolling turd! Not as bad as Tommy's Pontiac or Ford convertible, but close, very close. The Old's interior was ripped and filthy and every body panel, including the roof, was dented or distorted from some type of an encounter with an object that didn't give. If this car did in fact have only one owner as John said it did, it must have been previously owned by the "Kotchman Hell Drivers"!

John also felt compelled, as did Tommy, to paint a name on his car. He named it "The Rovin' Coffin"! Now I'm speculating here but maybe he chose that name because "Rusted-out Rovin' Piece of Dog Shit" wouldn't fit on the front fenders, What was he thinking??? Did he say to himself, "No point in taking any chances that a girl might actually want to go on a date with me in this piece of crap, I think I'll put a name on this car that will secure my fate in being as un-dateable as a Bridge Troll! Can you imagine some girl telling her father, "Oh Daddy, John is here to pick me up now, I'll see you later…if I live!" I can see the poor girl's father as he looks out the window and sees this horror show of a car with "Rovin' Coffin" painted on it! Actually, now that I think of it, that name was very appropriate for the car, because the interior smelled like someone had died in it!

If John's ownership of this car was some kind of a subliminal message about who he really was, then I thought, good luck John, better find a nice pillow to make out with at the drive-in! John even started to look different to us after seeing him with this car. He seemed to take on some of the car's persona, and eventually he evoked a similar reaction to a Chogie or Fat Joe sighting in that we would all scatter or make some excuse not to ride in his giant cootie catcher on wheels.

Tommy and John's cars were really at the extreme lower end of the "shit box" cars that were prevalent back then. Most of the junkers that were around weren't as bad as those three examples. There also were the in-between cars. By that I mean, they weren't new or newer model cars, and they weren't pieces of shit like Tommy or John's "scank-mobiles" either. Some of them were as old as my car, but had extensive work done to them either mechanically or cosmetically or both. These cars were still out of reach for my finances at the time and aside from that, I thought, if I had one of these, I would want to build it myself.

One such example of this type of car was owned by a kid I knew from school. His name was Joe Candon. I knew Joe since the seventh grade. He was a good natured, laid back kid that always got voted best looking or best dressed at school, but he didn't let it go to his head, so he was pretty easy to like.

One day while I was working at Paul's Mobil Joe Candon pulled in with his newly modified '57 Chevy Belair two-door hardtop. This car was one of the cleanest '57s I had ever seen at that time. It was all black with red and black factory interior and the car was in perfect condition. It had Crager S/S mag wheels, they really weren't mag (short for magnesium) wheels, they were steel, but all aftermarket wheels were referred to as mags by us. The front end of the car sat up several inches higher than stock from the addition of heavy-duty coil springs. Header dumps were peeking out from just behind the rear of the front fender wheel wells and you could hear the loping of a high performance cam along with the typewriter sound of solid mechanical lifters.

Joe pulled around to the side of the station and turned the car off. As it sat there I could hear the hot exhaust pipes and headers making metallic tinging sounds. Joe opened the hood and I saw two Carter AFB four-barrel carburetors sitting on an Offenhauser intake manifold and aluminum Corvette valve covers with tubular Doug's headers going through the inner fender panels.

Joe told me that he just put the car together and that it was a brand new 327 cubic inch 365 horsepower Corvette engine that he bought complete from carburetor to oil pan. He replaced the original four-barrel and manifold with the afore mentioned fuel delivery system. He stated that it also had a brand new "Muncie" close ratio four-speed and a new 4.56:1 posi-traction third member.

Wow, this was some car! I have to say I was more than a little jealous. After some more conversation Joe said his farewells, started the Chevy and pulled out on to Main Ave. heading towards Route 3. When he got part way through first gear he punched it to the floor and both rear tires broke loose leaving two heavy black strips on the road surface as the car "fish-tailed" back and forth down the roadway. These strips continued until he shifted to second gear, were they stopped for a few feet during gear change, and the started up again. The tires on that car smoked until he was completely out of sight! The two black strips went from Paul's lot, down Main Ave. to just short of Allwood Road (approximately two-hundred and fifty feet!)I was totally impressed after that display of power. Now Joe had all this in that Chevy and spent somewhere in the fifteen to eighteen hundred dollar range. That sounds cheap, but it was half or more of the price of a new car back then.

After Joe disappeared down Main Ave. with his Chevy that day, I never saw him or that car again. Sort of like the Cajun Queen. And just like the Cajun Queen, the image of that car stayed with me to this day. I did find out that the car was found in a garage in the early to mid seventies sometime after Joe's untimely death. Paul's nephew found the car intact and covered in dust. He brought it to Paul's, disassembled it, sold all the parts and then junked the body!! What a sad ending for a beautiful car.

After seeing Joe's '57 I made up my mind that someway, somehow I had to get into the high-performance game. Besides, all of my immediate friends started buying new or newer high or medium performance cars. Ted bought Joe Mattiello's '62 Chevy S/

S when Joe ordered a new '64 Chevy S/S. Ronnie bought a new black '63 Ford Galaxy 500 fast-back 390 cubic inch 300 horsepower, three-speed over-drive car. Tom bought an absolutely beautiful new Heritage Burgundy with black interior '63 Ford Galaxy 500XL fast-back with a 352 cubic inch 220 horsepower and a four-speed transmission and Swissy bought Danny Bray's 280 horsepower '61 Impala. It seemed that I was the only one with an older low-performance car. That is, not counting John Wry or Tommy Dione's four-wheeled disasters.

But, all that changed the day I bought Fred Schroeder's Oxford Blue '62 Ford 406 cubic inch 405 horsepower Galaxy two-door sedan. I finally moved up to the high-performance, newer car world, and it felt good, no, it felt great! The old '56 Ford was sold for one-hundred and twenty-five dollars to Matt Dywer, a Delawanna friend that had recently moved to Nutley. The last time I saw that '56 Ford, Matt was driving down Oak Street and turned onto River Road with a car load of girls, one of whom had half her body hanging out of the rear window flashing me by pulling up her top as Matt was blowing the horn and laughing! Hmm, maybe I should have kept that Ford, or moved to Nutley!

Chapter Twenty-Four:
Reality Sucks, Boy am I Steamed and Which Blew First!

One Sunday in late October or early November of 1964 a bunch of us went to Island Dragway to race our cars. Ted and George had their '62 Chevies, Ronnie had his '63 Ford and I had my 406 Ford. The first run down the track for my Ford was a wake-up call for me on the difference between the drag strip and the street in regards to traction and gearing and experience on a real drag strip.

I was running in A/S at the time and had my 8.50x15 Atlas Bucron tires on the rear with the 3:50 to1 one-legger (open) rear that I was running at the time while waiting to rebuild the original 4:11to1 "equa-loc" rear. I pulled up to the starting and found my opponent was to be a Black '63 Chevy Impala 327/250hp F/S car sponsored by Schwartz Chevrolet.

I didn't think too much about the competition at the time as I was a little nervous due to this being one of my first times running at an actual drag strip with my Ford and I was trying not to focus on all the spectators in the stands. But I do remember thinking, thank God it's only an F/stocker.

Well, the lights came down and this little Chevy jumped out at least two full open car lengths on me! I thought, holy shit! What the hell is this?! Anyway, instead of driving my Ford like I always did, I nailed the gas to the floor and I could feel the immediate loss of whatever traction I might have had. The little F/stocker then pulled another car length on me and, for a moment, instead of shifting to second gear, I shifted into panic mode. This was unlike most experiences I had on the street with this Ford that I felt I knew so well.

When I finally got my senses back, I lifted off the throttle until I felt that the rear wheel rotation matched the front wheel rotation. Once that happened, the Ford started to pull and I made my gear changes, from that point on, at the correct intervals. I then started to make up some lost ground on the little Chevy that I had a one-hundred and fifty-five horse-power advantage on, but I couldn't make up all of the lost real estate needed to win, and I crossed over the finish line one open car length behind the opponent that I was not originally all that concerned about.

When I picked up my time ticket it showed that I went 14.4 seconds at one-hundred and five miles per hour. Very poor E.T., but it did start to pull somewhat on the top end as I thought that mile per hour was more indicative of a mid thirteen second pass. The car had previously gone 13.2 seconds with the 4:11to1 rear and slicks when Fred ran it a year prior to this outing.

When I got back to the pits (if there was a rear exit at Island, I probably would have taken it and drove straight home) Roy told me my right rear tire went "up in smoke," which I surmised as it was happening. I realized I should not have been racing the car that day with the open rear and decided not to give in to the urge to race it on the track again until I had the 4:11's back in the car. No point in racing if the car isn't up to it's full potential, I rationalized. Plus my ego was already wounded enough by the little F/Stock Chevy that "cleaned my clock." Live and learn.

Ted ran his '62 327/300hp car that was formerly owned by Joe Mattiello. He made a few passes with the Nassau Blue Chevy running in the E/stock class. The car ran in the low 15 second range all day long; Well not all day, just until Ted blew the transmission!

Oh man this really sucks the bird, we all thought. We wondered, how in the hell are we going to get it home now? That is one of the things none of us considered at all when we drove the cars to the track instead of towing them. But, we were all just barely able to afford the cars themselves, let alone another car to tow with! There-in lies the difference between serious strip racers that have money or sponsored backing and half-assed street racers like us with no racing budget at all.

Anyway, we got permission to park the car by the drag strip owner's house, which was up on the hill adjacent to and within eye-shot of the track. So that is what we did. Later that week Ted got someone with a tow truck to fetch the car and bring it to Paul's where we would complete the repairs.

Ted picked up a good used trans. and one day after work we pushed the car up onto Paul's lift to begin the transmission replacement. It was a hard sell to Paul at first, because Paul said, "Every-time he (meaning Ted) comes around, something happens!" Paul was referring to incidents like the time Ted came into Paul's with the '62 and said it was over-heating. I told Paul I'd take a look at it and he said, "Go ahead, but for Christ's sake be careful!" I assured Paul that I would be careful and that he didn't have to worry, because I felt that I knew what I was doing by this time. But, that opinion was from my nineteen year-old minds perception and Paul had a whole different way of seeing the possible out-come of anything we did because in his fifty-year old mind's perception he knew that I/we couldn't assure anyone of anything, we usually were not careful and we really didn't know exactly what we were doing…yet. He absolutely had every right to worry.

So, with Paul's words still ringing in my ears, Ted and I walked over to the '62, opened the hood and then I very carefully and slowly removed the radiator cap with a shop rag, all the while keeping as much of my face and body at the furthest distance from the car as I could.

Now with the cap removed we observed some light steam gently flowing from the radiator filler spout. I told Ted to stay back for a while and did the same myself. After a minute or so I felt it was safe enough to look in and check the water level.

On the way back from the hospital later that morning Paul said, "See, do ya see what I mean? That's why I'm always tell you guys to be careful, but you always say, "Don't worry, don't worry I know what I'm doing." "Don't worry my God-damned ass!"

I was fairly lucky as my eyes closed from natural instinct and I only suffered minor steam burns around them and one side of my face. Apparently there was an air or steam pocket in the radiator that held back the "geyser" that erupted shortly after I looked in. I didn't know about air pockets then, but I do now...just like Paul did then!

However, even with those perceptions in his thoughts Paul still allowed us to use the lift to replace Ted's transmission. When we put it on the lift we saw ice coming from the holes in the block where the freeze-out plugs used to be! Oh shit, this is not good! It turns out Ted did not winterize his car yet, (I'm not sure what he was waiting for) and it got a lot colder up in the mountains of Hackettstown than we/he ever anticipated.

Well, the car thawed out after several hours in the warm garage bay and after replacing the freeze-out plugs we filled it with coolant, checked for leaks, of which there were none. That part of the repair was not anticipated, but it seemed to be completed. Now that we were reasonably sure the engine was ok, we replaced the transmission, which only took about forty-five minutes to do. Everything went well with that repair also. Then we put the car back on the ground and Ted went to back it out of the bay, but it would not move and we also heard a loud metallic clanging sound coming from the rear-end. What the hell was this now?! Paul came over and said, "You dumb bastards, you replaced the transmission and the whole time you had a blown rear!"

I thought that was impossible, I knew the transmission was bad. Paul walked away shaking his head and making all sorts of unintelligible comments. Ted and I quickly removed the side cover from the three-speed and looked inside; Sure enough, the trans. was toast! What the hell was the story here, we wondered. We called Paul over and after he looked inside, he said, "Well you're right it is blown, so you must have blown the rear too." Either that, or someone stole the rear, but if they did that, they wouldn't have gone through the trouble of putting the blown one back; At least I didn't think so.

We put the car back on the lift and inspected the rear-end area. There was no evidence that someone tampered with it at all. We then pulled the rear and found it to also be blown. "How in the hell could that happen?," I asked Paul. He said, "With you guys, anything is possible!"

We ran over to Joe Mattiello's house and grabbed the 3:36 to1 rear that came out of his '64 Super Sport when we installed a brand new 4:56 posi third-member. Within an hour Ted's '62 was back on the road again. I gave up wondering how this freak incident occurred as it made now sense to me then or now. I sum it all up in a saying my friend Mike Beldowicz used to use when something unexplainable occurs. He used to say: "Such are the defugalties of life." It really has no real meaning, at least not in Webster's Dictionary that I could find, but saying it works for me in cases like this and it really doesn't need to be explained any further. Ted's trip to the track cost him a transmission, a rear-end and almost an engine!

Chapter Twenty-Five:
Quick Fords and a Slow Chevy

We went to school with many of the "Surrey Lane Boys" (Allwood section of Clifton) and got along pretty well with all of them, of which there were about six or seven. We used to drive to Surrey Lane on occasion to "shoot-the-shit" with them, mainly about cars. Sometimes we would have a race or two with them just for fun. We would also meet them at Rutt's and other car cruise places from time-to-time, but we usually never went anywhere with them aside from that, because we realized early on that they strayed a little over the line from what we were willing to get involved in. Nothing real bad (that I knew of), just more than we were willing to do.

One incident involving them was when one of them, Nevin, was about to have his beautiful Heritage Burgandy '63 Ford Galaxy 500 fast-back 427 cubic inch, 425 horse-power car repossessed at the same time Pete needed an engine to replace his car's worn-out 390 cubic inch 375 horsepower engine in his '61 Ford Fairlane tudor sedan. So, before Nevin's car was repossessed, they swapped engines. They also swapped out the intake manifold, valve covers and any other detectable items just before the '63 got confiscated with that worn-out old "390" in place of the very powerful 427 engine it came with! Some poor guy along the line got a beautiful, although very under-powered and worn-out 1963 427 Ford.

At this time period I had been racing my 406 Ford a year and a half and I grew weary of the cost to keep it on the road and keep racing it due to the amount of parts breakage, mostly because of my driving technique, which was a little to aggressive for a street driven car. Actually it was a little too aggressive for any car, street or track. I should have never been "full-throttle shifting" a three-speed column shifted car with the torque the 406 had in the first place. That was the main cause of the drive train components failing like they did. That and over winding the engine by relying on a shitty little "Dixco" tachometer that I really couldn't see all that well and had questionable accuracy. (No, I did not take any lesson's from Jack Jorg, "Speed-Shift King"!) The big difference between Jack and me is that I only broke my own parts and my car was actually stick-shift!

Well anyway, I decided it was time to get something a little more conservative. First came a terrible decision on my part to take a partial trade-in of a '58 Plymouth fury with a 426 cubic inch 360 horsepower "street wedge" motor. After a very brief ownership, I sold this car and burned any photographs or forensic proof that I actually owned it. I tried to convince my friends that they must have been mistaken in their assumption that it was ever mine in the first place!

I then focused on building a '57 Chevy Two-Ten two door sedan that I bought from some thief that I knew from Passaic. It was a six cylinder automatic that didn't run, but all-in-all the body and interior were decent and the price of seventy-five dollars was acceptable. First I made sure the car wasn't stolen. Surprisingly it

wasn't. Then Roy and I towed it home. The thief offered to tow it
to my house, but I declined, as I didn't want him to know where I
lived for obvious reasons.

A couple of years before this purchase, one of the thief's friends
had ordered a brand new Ermine White '63 Chevy Impala with the
409/ 425 horsepower engine and a four-speed. Around the time it
was due to come in he was driving past the dealership that he
ordered it from, and saw it sitting in the lot, or at least he assumed
it was his car. He went back later that night, after they were closed,
and stole the twin four-barrel intake manifold and the distributor
from the car, still unsure if it was his or not. The next day the
salesman called to tell him the car was in, but, he said, "There is a
slight problem; somebody stole the intake manifold and we had to
order you a new one!" The thief was elated and said to his friends,
"Now I have two of them…just in case." So, all things considered,
when he offered to tow the car home for me I said, "I think I'll tow
the car home myself…just in case!"

Anyway, the first thing I did when I got the car home was to take the
engine and transmission out and "eighty-six" them both. I then bought
a complete 283 cubic inch engine with a "Duntov 098" solid lifter cam
that was in need of a rebuild (my first mistake). Actually buying the
engine wasn't a bad idea, but rebuilding it the way I did was. My friend
Mike Beldowicz and I honed out the block and cut the cylinder ridge
way more than we should have. It really should have been bored out.

One Saturday morning during the build-up process Mike, Roy
and I went to the meadowlands in North Arlington / Kearny where
there resided approximately ten junk yards in a row. My intention
was to find all the parts I needed to make the car stick-shift. It had
to be stick-shift. No ifs-ands-or-buts about it.

We stopped at Bib's, the first yard we came to, walked into the
office and I told the guy what I was looking for. He said, "Come

with me," so we followed him into the yard where he took us over to a clean little '55 Chevy Belair two-door sedan. He said the motor was bad and I could buy all the stick parts from this car and as an added plus, it had a floor-shift already in place. The car was otherwise in very nice condition and it's dark green paint still shined very well. My first thought was, maybe I should take the whole car, because it appeared to be better than the '57 I was doing, but I had already started the project and felt committed to it. This poor decision, along with many other behavioral characteristics that my friends and I exhibited, must have had something to do with riding through the mosquito spray so many years before.

In spite of any conflicting thoughts I might started having, I made a deal with the guy to take all of the stick parts that I needed from the '55 for forty-five dollars. We then went to Mike's car to get the tools needed to strip the parts and asked the yard owner if he had a jack that we could use. He told us he'd be right back and returned in several minutes with a large fork lift truck. He asked us to move to the side so we wouldn't get hurt. He then placed the forks under the driver's side of the car and flipped it over onto it's roof! Even back then I thought that it was a shame to destroy a car like that. That car, judging it by today's standards, and using the one to ten scale, was definitely about a seven or eight in considering the condition of the body and interior.

Anyway, after I finished rebuilding the engine and completed the change over to stick shift, I put the '57 on the road as a daily driver initially using three-two barrel carburetors and a three-speed (floor shifted) transmission. Actually, back then every car was a daily driver unless you had the money to have a street car and a track car, which I didn't and most other kids didn't either. It was hard enough just keeping one car on the road and using it for the occasional trip to the track or route 21.

As it turned out, I didn't have to worry about racing this car, because as time would tell it was a "rat" (meaning it wasn't very quick). It was very dependable though and, all things considered, maybe I was better off this way; At least I wouldn't be tempted to race it.

Months later when my friend Mike Beldowicz took his D/ Gas '57 Chevy apart I bought the four-speed, the dual quads and the 4:88 to1 rear and installed all of those parts in my Chevy hoping to improve it's performance. As it turned out, even thought it was quicker than before, I basically made it a faster "rat"! I realized years later that I probably lost a lot of compression by cutting the ridge and honing it as extremely as we did.

Mike's '57 Chevy was a Belair two-door sedan with a Rochester fuel injected small block which was later changed to "dual quads"(two four-barrel carbs). We (Mike and I) ran this car in the D/Gas class to fair success, mainly because it was a very consistent car. I usually drove the car due to Mike having a nervous eye problem. It ran 13.9 to 14.0 seconds, which was not great for a D/ Gasser, but, as I stated, it was very consistent and that accounted for a lot.

Mike bought the '57 from Bev's (my girlfriend at the time, and soon to be wife) cousin Dennis. Dennis sold it to buy another '57. This one, would be a Belair two-door hardtop with a small block and a four-speed. Dennis was almost relegated to buying a Corvair or some other low performance car after being caught blasting down Main Ave. by his and Bev's Aunt Fan one evening. Aunt Fan was visiting a friend, who just happened to live in Delawanna, and while they were standing in front of the friends house saying their goodbyes they heard, as she put it, "The squealing of tires and a deafening roar coming towards them." Aunt Fan said to her friend, "Look at this maniac coming down the street"! Then, as the green

'57 Belair passed by with Dennis concentrating on the tachometer and nothing else, she exclaimed to her friend, "Oh my God, it's my nephew Dennis!" She re-told that story many times over the years, God rest her soul.

Although I have a fairly good long-term memory, I can't remember one single race with my '57 Chevy. Maybe that's a good thing, because if, in fact, I did race it at all, my mind will not allow me to recall it. Just as well, as it's always best not to dwell on the negative aspects of life. Even though it was hard to build a small-block Chevy that didn't go, I managed to do so with this car. It sure looked good though. Can't win them all I guess.

Chapter Twenty-Six:
Epilogue

I kept that '57 Chevy until August of 1966 when my wife Bev and I purchased a brand new Wimbledon White 1966 Ford Fairlane GTA with black interior and a 390 cubic inch 335 horsepower engine. (I raced this car on the street and at the track whenever I could sneak it away from Bev.)

I sold the Chevy for four-hundred and twenty-five dollars with all the parts I mentioned previously still intact. Within one month it was in a junk yard totaled out! I had my reservations about the kid that bought it as he seemed like a real dip-shit and I guess I was right. Too bad about that old Chevy. But cars like that one were cheap back then and there was one on every corner.

Along with the Fairlane, Bev and I had a clean white '55 Chevy Belair two-door hardtop with a '62 283 cubic inch engine and a three-speed column shift. I bought this Chevy at a car lot in Wallington, NJ for one-hundred and seventy-five dollars plus I traded in a worn-out '55 Chevy four-door six cylinder automatic that Bev got for free from an Aunt of hers. We ran this Chevy for several years, then my father took it and after several months under his ownership, the body looked like a golf ball, but it still ran well for several more years after!

The list of cars I have owned since then would fill a book itself. Lot's of hot rods, muscle cars, antique cars, race cars and even some that were actually used for family conveyance.

Recently in talking over the old times with my friend Larry, I said that if I had a choice as to what time period I would like to live in, if I could do it all over again, I thought maybe the 1940s might have been the best era of all to be living in the United States of America with all things considered. But Larry's position was that the best era to be alive in was the era that we (him and I) came from, the 1950s and 1960s. To bolster his belief in that opinion he stated to me that we had the best cars, the best music, the best styles, good education, good medical services, a good economy and most of all a good, learned respect of others. We also had good work ethics and we didn't expect hand-outs or anything at all that we didn't earn. We earned everything we got and we learned from the people of the "Greatest Generation"; our parents, relatives, teachers and neighbors!

It didn't take much thinking for me to agree completely with Larry's thoughts on this subject. We did grow-up in the best era *ever!* So, now I no longer romanticize about other times. I now just wish I could live my life over in the same exact time period I did live it in...only slower! Larry is one-hundred percent correct in his theory; The decade of 1955 to 1965 was absolutely the best of times! Just ask anyone who lived in it with us.

I blame most of the adventures, misadventures and obsessions described in this book on riding our bikes through the mosquito spray years earlier. I believe it was D.D.T. not A.D.D. that accounted for some of the "revoltin' developments" described here within!

I have to go now as I started wiring my '37 Chevy coupe after putting it off for the last twenty-eight years, besides, I can see a light illuminating from inside the car, I must have left my TL122D turned on under the dash.